NEW RUSSIAN DESIGN
CONSTANTIN BOYM

КОНСТАНТИН БОЙМ
НОВЫЙ РУССКИЙ ДИЗАЙН

NEW RUSSIAN DESIGN
CONSTANTIN BOYM

RIZZOLI
NEW YORK

TO MY GRANDMOTHER, ROSA GRINBERG

First published in the United States of America in 1992 by
Rizzoli International Publications, Inc.
300 Park Avenue South
New York, NY 10010

Copyright © 1992 Rizzoli International Publications
Text copyright © 1992 Constantin Boym

Library of Congress Cataloging-in-Publication Data

Boym, Constantin.
New Russian design / Constantin Boym.
p. cm.
Includes bibliographical references and index.
ISBN 0-8478-1613-3
1. Design—Soviet Union—History—20th century. I. Title.
NK1456.A1B68 1992
745.4'4947'0904—dc20   92–7329
                                                CIP

Designed by José Conde

This book was typeset in Adobe Garamond, News Gothic, Garsans, and
Constantfont, a typeface based on letters designed by Alexander Gelman

Printed in Singapore

CONTENTS

In his book *Mythologies,* Roland Barthes wrote: "Faced with anything foreign, the Established Order knows only two types of behavior, which are both mutilating: either to acknowledge it as a Punch and Judy show, or to defuse it as a pure reflection of the West." One challenge in writing about Russian design is avoiding either of these two extremes of misrepresentation. Obviously, the subject must be placed in a social and historical framework. But how is one to incorporate the necessary information without making the book an encyclopedia? How to transmit the complex web of cultural connotations, references, and precedents in this work—a web further tangled by the long practice of ideological double-speak? How to share all the excitement and pessimism, the hope and fear that I encountered in the course of researching this book during a hard Russian winter in 1990–1991?

Searching for an appropriate approach and format, I came to think of the book as a mosaic—a bit-by-bit portrait comprising profiles of designers, historical information, social commentary, and excursuses into art criticism. This concept, representative of Russia's own fragmentation and confusion, would give the reader a sense of the heterogeneous nature of Russian culture. On the other hand, it would extend an invitation to a further inquiry into various aspects of the history of Russian economics, design, or art. This format is also appropriate for a work dealing with a situation in the process of dynamic development. Never intended to be an exhaustive academic study, this book is based on necessary selective research. Some degree of subjectivity is perhaps unavoidable in a book written by a practicing designer.

The book's title is self-explanatory at first glance; nevertheless, each word requires some clarifications. First of all, how new is the "new Russian design"? The original idea was to present only works created in the atmosphere of Mikhail Gorbachev's reforms; in short, the design since perestroika. Preliminary study, however, proved that most design ideas and projects of the late 1980s originated, in one form or another, in the beginning of the decade. Thus, the main body of the book is devoted, generally, to the last ten years of Russia's cultural history. The age of the designers featured in the essays ranges from mid-twenties to late forties. Those who started working back in the 1960s are included provided that their output during the last decade has been timely and relevant. It should be noted that design in Russia is not generally a field for child prodigies: many of the field's leading figures found their true calling after numerous career changes and personal crises.

This book originally was started under the title *New Soviet Design.* After the explosive political events of 1991, an amazed world witnessed the disintegration of the USSR as a single unified state. In spite of cooperation, and economic and military ties among some of the former republics, the former union, along with its name, has passed into history. The term "Soviet" in the state name, to be sure, has long lost its original meaning, that of "a council of the people's deputies"; it has come to be used as an identifying tag based on historical tradition. I retained the word "Soviet" in the descriptions of the events and the projects up to the year 1991. Since all the designers but one featured here come from the capital and its surrounding regions, I have decided to term their current and future work as "Russian" design. (In fact, the book could also be called *New Moscow Design.*)

The most important concern, finally, is whether new Russian design should be regarded as design at all. An American reader, in particular, will question the inclusion of certain works, which are at best marginal with regard to a conventional framework for Western design discourse. A comparative analysis of Eastern and Western design—of their goals, methods, and practice—is an interesting subject, one that lies beyond the scope of this book. The reader will see that since the 1920s, Russian design has evolved as a multidisciplinary cultural effort rather than as a market-oriented, professional tool; throughout its history, it has remained a visionary rather than a service discipline. This orientation has been a mixed blessing. On the one hand, design has effectively functioned as a critique, as a personalized, idealistic trajectory pointed at the positive transformation of Russian society; on the other, new design has been largely ignored by the industry and the marketplace and has never had a chance to affect the Soviet economy, the misery of which has now been revealed to the world. Not surprisingly, in Russia the public still perceives design as a superfluous, visionary activity.

Some readers might find my views pessimistic. In fact, they are full of hope compared with those expressed in contemporary Russian periodicals. The Western liberal tradition has long tended to idealize many aspects of Russian life, culture, and society. Even today one finds leaflets that lament the demise of Socialism and Communism. Some Westerners still refuse to accept that Russia today is going through an unprecedented process of cleansing, of reevaluating its goals and objectives, of getting onto new, sound foundations—and that this process is painful. I believe that the controversies surrounding this unique historical moment should be exposed openly, in the best tradition of glasnost, and excessive nostalgia and emotional responses are simply irrelevant.

This book would not be possible without the enthusiastic cooperation of all Russian designers featured here, who generously shared their time and creative resources with me. Specifically, I would like to thank Vladimir Chaika in Moscow and Leonid Yentus in New York, who spent many lengthy sessions telling me about the people and events on the Moscow design scene. I want to thank design critics Oleg Genisaretsky and Sergey Smirnov and architect Evgeny Asse for giving me valuable insights into the contemporary design situation, and Svetlana Strizhnova, director of the Mayakovsky Museum in Moscow, for an inspiring tour of that valuable institution.

I have to thank my parents in Moscow for putting up with me during my stay, and my friend, architect Evgeny Monakhov, for taking me around and for making a difficult trip easier.

In New York, I want to express my gratitude to the editors of the magazine *ID,* Annetta Hanna and Chee Pearlman, who back in 1988 commissioned me to write an article on Soviet design. Without their encouragement, this book would not have been possible.

Thanks are due also to: Laurene Leon, for her help and support; Vitaly Komar, Alex Melamid, Vladimir Kanevsky, and Tom Nugent, for their information and advice; Susan Yelavich of the Cooper-Hewitt Museum, for giving me the opportunity to present portions of this work at a symposium in New York City; and Robert Janjigian, my editor at Rizzoli, for his encouragement and patience. I am also grateful to José Conde, the designer of the book, for his dedicated and inspiring work—against all odds.

9

1917–1932

In 1988, graduates of high schools throughout the Soviet Union were happy: they had one less final exam to take. Oral examinations in the history of the USSR had been suspended, as few teachers could tackle the sudden and unexpected controversy surrounding their once-familiar subject. At that time the policy of glasnost, or public openness, was reaching new heights, and ever more information was being revealed about the gruesome details of seventy years of Communist Party rule. That information, finally made accessible to the public, overturned all established criteria. The matter was becoming increasingly clear: the whole history of the country would have to be rewritten and rethought before it could be presented to the judgment of the next generation.

Obviously, the history of Russian design has been affected by the changing interpretation of the country's historical background. Varying opinions are being voiced about virtually every stage of its development. Such differences can be traced to the years before glasnost. As recently as the 1960s, activities of the early Russian avant-garde were not considered a part of official design history. Soviet critics argued that revolutionary artists and architects did not work for the market, and that "their projects were intended to fulfill the needs of the Soviet people through noncommercial relationships." Thus, the avant-garde artists who proposed "romantic programs for the total renewal of life and material environment" were to be considered outside of mainstream design discourse.[1] Indeed, hardly a single project by any of the avant-garde masters was produced on an industrial scale. "The clothing designs proposed by Constructivist artists for mass production were at best made up in one copy only and worn as the artist's personal dress; the furniture designed under the supervision of Tatlin and Lissitzky as academic exercises was gradually destroyed in the storerooms . . . ; the interior designs of Rodchenko,

the Steinberg brothers, and others were used only in exhibitions of the contemporary look; china designs seldom went further than the drawing board, and so on," states Anatolii Strigalev.[2] Yet the artists of the 1920s did more than establish a unique and characteristic style for their time. "In the ontology of culture, intentions have no less importance than their realization," wrote art historian Igor Golomstock.[3] The manifestoes and theoretical concepts of the twenties still reverberate in arguments at design conferences. Indeed, even though the avant-garde was nearly forbidden in the Soviet Union for many years, its legacy remains an important reference point for contemporary designers there. In this respect, it is necessary to look in more detail at the theory and practice of the development in the 1920s.

The movements known as Production Art and Constructivism deserve attention among the diverse and controversial creative tendencies of the time. The postulates of Production Art were first formulated on the pages of the avant-garde newspaper *Art of the Commune* in December of 1918. In the first issue, an editorial declared that "art is like any other means of production," and that "a real object is the aim of true creativity." A distinction between the new goals and the crafts tradition was made clear by Nikolai Punin: "Art for the proletariat is not a sacred temple for lazy contemplation, but work, a factory, producing completely artistic objects."[4] The Productivists were not interested in the object in the Duchampian sense. They called for an industrial production of useful, necessary things, with an artist being an organizer, and a worker—"a conscious and active participant in the creative process."[5] Essentially, the task was to do more than make well-designed objects. Productivists wanted to redesign life itself; by education and personal example, they aspired to bring about a utopian state of universal, collective creativity, accessible to everyone. This sentiment went hand in hand with the reigning ideological policies, and as

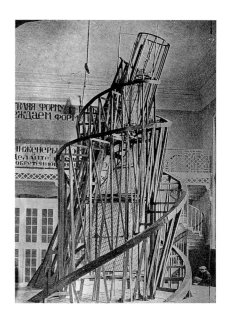

Right: Vladimir Tatlin, *Monument to the Third International*, 1920, model.

such, it gained wide support from the nascent Soviet government, especially in the initial period of 1918–21.

Conventional artistic activity, such as painting or sculpture, was not forbidden within the Production Art movement, but was relegated to the role of "laboratory work," an exercise for an imminent future application in the field of industry. The criteria for successful formal experimentation in the arts was, in fact, based on simplicity and economy of construction, and on the skillful handling of readily available industrial materials. Thus, Boris Arvatov argued that "an artist who had no knowledge of working with materials was utterly meaningless in a factory."[6] The Third Exhibition of the Society of

Above: Alexander Rodchenko, *Oval Hanging Construction No. 12*, 1920–21. This work was featured in the Third Exhibition of the Society of Young Artists, Moscow, 1921.

Young Artists (the OBMOKhU) in Moscow in May 1921 featured a number of expressive works, constructed according to the principles of Productivism. Free-standing constructions were made of standard metal shapes, held together by welding and wire trusses, which took their inspiration from utilitarian mechanical devices and engineering structures.

A highly influential work for all Productivist artists was the *Monument to the Third International* by

Vladimir Tatlin, first exhibited as a model in November 1920. The proposed colossal, 1350-foot-high spiral structure was intended to house three glass volumes that were to rotate at variable speed. For presentation, the model of the tower was surrounded by slogans, calling for collaborative effort on the part of various professional trades, together with the artist-constructor, in the creation of "a new form in honor of the Third International."[7] The emphasis on collective production and the striking impact of the work's innovative structural aesthetics made Tatlin's tower "as significant for its period as the Eiffel Tower had been for the end of the nineteenth century."[8]

By 1921, the Production Art movement had regrouped under the banner of Constructivism. The original founders—Alexei Gan, Alexander Rodchenko, and Varvara Stepanova—were joined by the Steinberg brothers, Alexandr Vesnin, Liubov Popova, Gustav Klucis, and the other artists and architects. The activities of the group were divided along two general lines. One was related to teaching at the recently established VKhUTEMAS (Higher Art and Technical Studios). The aim of this state-supported school, as noted in the resolution signed by Lenin, was "to train artists of high quality for the benefit of the national economy."[9] This connection between art and economy required the education of a new type of artist, one well versed in Constructivist ideals. "Theoretical discussions and studio practice

were intended to produce a model for an 'art engineer' or 'art constructor,' an originator who was prepared to work with others and was familiar with strict logic."[10] Of particular importance was the Wood and Metalworking Faculty, headed by Rodchenko. He recalled how "out of the same department which once made mounts for icons, lamps, and other church plate, there began to emerge constructors, producing electrical devices, metal objects of daily use, and metal furniture."[11] Unfortunately, this program—a forerunner of true industrial design education in Russia—had an even shorter life span than the Bauhaus, and was completely reorganized by 1930.

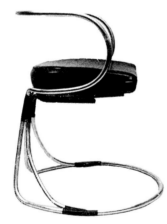

The other part of the Constructivists' activity was aimed at the practical implementation of their theoretical concepts. Their attempts to merge "art into life," however, were met with great resistance, both by the industries and by the public at large. The New Economic Policy (NEP) was introduced in 1921, aimed at revitalizing the Soviet economy, which had been decimated by war. The policy allowed for limited private enterprise within a state-controlled system. The taste of the new entrepreneurial class— the potential clients and buyers of new products—

was rooted in prerevolutionary eclectic aesthetics. Soviet government organizations supported Constructivism as a concept, but in practical matters showed far more traditional aesthetic attitudes. Thus when Vladimir Tatlin approached the New Lessner Factory in Petrograd with ideas for creative production, he was effectually turned down.[12] A more successful area of collaboration with industries occurred in the field of textile design. Popova and Stepanova started to work at the Tsindel Textile Print Factory in 1923. There they produced numerous trademark Constructivist patterns, all based on combinations of simple geometrical figures and primary colors. A year later, a contemporary reviewer wrote, "All Moscow was wearing fabrics of Popova's design, without even knowing it."[13] Yet in 1925, Stepanova reported: "Drawings reminiscent of the town and industry, for example—those featuring straight lines and circles—are not being made now. [The buyers] are accepting only drawings recalling the countryside: streams and flowers."[14]

Since the eighteenth century, Russian political events and sentiments had been recorded on ceramics. So in 1918, when Sergey Chekhonin became an art director of the nationalized Imperial Porcelain Factory, he found it appropriate to apply the ardor of revolutionary art to ceramic plates. It was a matter of decorating rather than design, since the artists had to use the stock of white wares, left from the reign of the last Russian czars.[15] In 1922 an avant-garde group of Suprematists, headed by Kazimir Malevich, got involved in work at the factory. The stark-white porcelain and brilliant primary color glazes of the tableware made an ideal medium for their abstract compositions. Malevich and Suetin (who later became a factory art director) soon made a series of designs for experimental teapots, cups, and vases. "All things, all our world should be dressed in the Suprematic shapes: fabrics, wallpaper, pots, plates, furniture, and street signs," wrote Malevich.[16] The

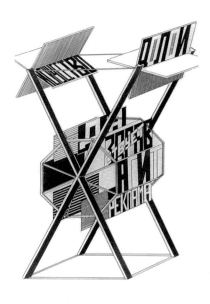
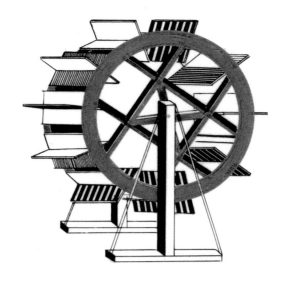

Above: Gustav Klucis, Designs for "Radio Announcers" and propaganda kiosks, 1922.

artists applied their theoretical principles to a wide array of everyday objects, aspiring to a further interaction between art and life. Thus, a series of inkstands took the shape of Malevich's horizontal architectural composition, *Architekton*. Although they were seen as powerful formal symbols of avant-garde design, Suprematist ceramics had an emblematic fate as well: they remained prototypes and never went into production.

In the absence of practical commissions from the industrial sector, many Constructivists continued experimental work in graphics and environmental design that could be used as revolutionary propaganda. In 1922 Gustav Klucis designed a series of agit-constructions, intended to decorate the festivities of the fifth anniversary of the October Revolution. Called "Radio Announcers," the structures actually combined several functions, containing loudspeaker, screen, podium for public speeches, and display stand for books and newspapers. At least two of these were built in Moscow, generating extraordinary attention.[17] Klucis's projects provided certain formulas that would later become typical features in Constructivist design:

multifunctionality, transformation and folding capability, and an economical and undisguised expression of construction and materials.

These concepts were developed further by Alexander Rodchenko in his project for the interior of the Workers' Club, exhibited at an International Exhibition in Paris in 1925. Workers' Clubs were regarded by the Soviet government as important elements in the cultural and ideological indoctrination of the masses. As social centers they were supposed to replace the church and to remove the worker from the harmful individualistic influence of the family. Not surprisingly, the Soviets allocated valuable resources for creating and exhibiting Rodchenko's canonical work of Russian Constructivism on French soil.

Rodchenko applied the principles of structural economy in his use of space and in his construction of each furniture piece. "An object designed for its dynamism has a greater number of potential uses and is better suited to modern living conditions," he claimed.[18] In order to express dynamism, some objects were designed to be collapsible for easy removal and

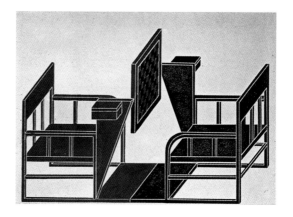

storage. Others had movable parts, like the chess table with rotating chessboard, or the reading table with hinged leaves. Juxtaposition of elementary geometric forms—circle, triangle, and square—also contributed to a visual dynamics of the environment. The most ingenious pieces were also multifunctional, such as one work that unfolded into an elegant composition containing a screen, bench, and display board. Of course, it was not mere economy that made the designer incorporate multiple uses into the simple shapes of his furniture. An echo of the Productivist creed reverberated in Rodchenko's work: to reduce the number of objects in the human environment, to rethink and simplify the material qualities of everyday life.

Even though the furniture for the Workers' Club was made in France, Rodchenko specified that it be made of wood, as that was the only widely available material in Russia at the time. Vladimir Tatlin's designs also made ingenious use of wood. "In the West the reform of furniture is under way, through the use of bicycle tubing in design," wrote Tatlin in 1925, referring to the experiments of Mies van der Rohe and Marcel Breuer. "We have also had some attempts of this kind. But we lack the necessary material—steel tubing."[19] Tatlin suggested bentwood as an economical and functional substitute, and used it in his design of a sled frame. "The wood sled is much lighter than steel: one can carry it on one's shoulder, and it is pleasant to touch in winter, since it

doesn't freeze," he observed. In 1923 Tatlin produced remarkably pragmatic designs for clothing, which he attempted to put into production. John Milner noted, "His designs were necessarily the opposite of applied art, for no art as such was here applied; there was no trace of decoration. Tatlin was in effect reinventing the coat, stove, and suit. These designs contained no rhetoric of style or self-expression."[20]

In the late 1920s, Tatlin's uncompromising position contrasted with that of many of his colleagues. While at work on models for his man-powered glider, the aging avant-garde master reproached the artists who he believed had abandoned the ideals of Constructivism. Indeed, by that time Rodchenko, Lissitzky, Klucis, Stepanova, and many others had largely forsaken large-scale industrial work and had devoted themselves to work in book, advertising, and poster design. Together, these designers revolutionized graphic art. Thanks to their innovations in type, layout, composition, and color, they created the characteristic look of the Russian avant-garde. The principles they employed in the field of graphics derived from, and provided a visual manifestation of, the Constructivist concept of industrial production. "Our palette is a well-equipped, contemporary printing press," said Lissitzky of his working method.[21] Photomontage, with an expressive and dynamic combination of typographic and pictorial images, became a trademark Constructivist devise, developed by

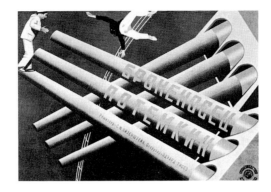

Rodchenko and perfected by Klucis. The photograph, well-suited to mechanical reproduction, satisfied the designers' commitment to technology and to an economical means of production. At the same time, it presented a way of using figurative imagery without falling back into pictorial realism.

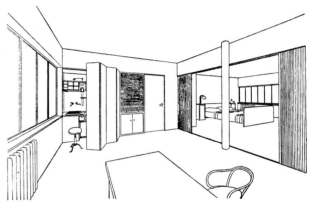

Perhaps the most significant and controversial Constructivist developments took place in the field of architecture. Since the early 1920s, many architects had eagerly accepted the program of Production Art, and were committed to architecture as "a useful art," an instrument for building a better future and a new way of life. Accordingly, the goals and methods of practicing architecture had to be re-defined. Moisei Ginzburg, a theoretician and architect, considered Constructivism a social position, a means of building "new relationships in labor and everyday life."[22] Functional, rather than aesthetic, goals constituted the main task of the new architecture, and accordingly, functionalism became its working method. Architects began to take a pragmatic, problem-solving approach, analogous with that of the inventor. The machine served as their model, because "through the activity of all working parts, and the total absence of idle elements, it naturally brings forward a concept of Constructivism."[23] Factories and industrial complexes presented another model with their "prosaic earnestness and everyday reality." Ironically, Ginzburg, a Communist, found

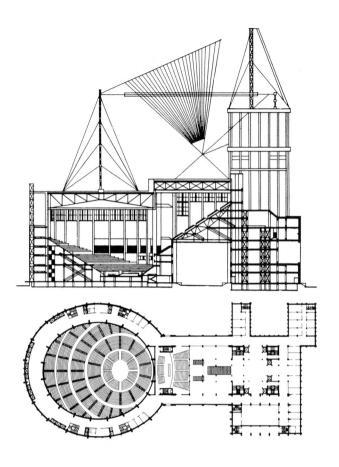

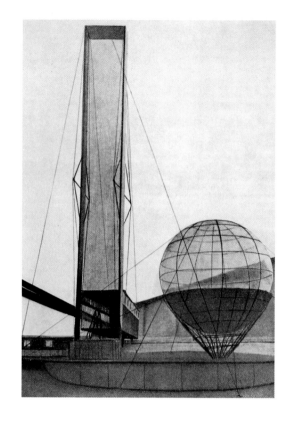

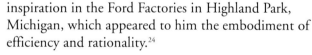

Top and above: Vesnin brothers, competition design for *Palace of Labor*, Moscow, 1923, section and plan.

Above right: Ivan Leonidov, *Lenin Institute*, 1927, model.

Below: Ilya Golosov, *Zuev Workers' Club*, Moscow, 1927–29.

inspiration in the Ford Factories in Highland Park, Michigan, which appeared to him the embodiment of efficiency and rationality.[24]

Industrial architecture helped develop a formal language of Constructivism and a characteristic palette of materials: concrete, steel, and glass. Ginzburg repeatedly emphasized that Constructivism had to remain a working method, not a style, and that no predetermined aesthetics were appropriate for its true followers. He wrote, "Form is an unknown function, X, that has to be solved anew each time, like any other unknown."[25] However, as the movement evolved, it went in quite a different direction. Successful and original projects, such as the offices for *Leningrad Pravda* newspaper (1924) or the ARKOS Company Building (1924) by the Vesnin brothers, made Constructivism a fashionable and much imitated architectural style. As many architects switched to the Constructivist idiom, mediocre and outdated compositional ideas began to be dressed in trendy glass-and-concrete skin, compromising the entire movement. Established masters of prerevolutionary architecture also took up the new

style, contributing their own high-quality, yet inevitably watered-down interpretations.

By the end of the 1920s, many original Constructivists were engaged in solving practical architectural problems, such as those related to the implementation of the first Five Year Plan. They fought against meaningless canonization of their own principles through the publications of the Organization of Soviet Architects (OSA), and engaged in an ongoing professional debate, the fierceness of which is difficult to overestimate. The rise of such masters as Ivan Leonidov, a so-called poet of pure form, brought renewed life to the Constructivist cause. Le Corbusier called him "the hope of Russian Architectural Constructivism."[26] Leonidov's stunning compositions of simple geometric volumes, such as the Lenin Institute (1927) or the House of Heavy Industry (1929–30), offered a new direction for modern architecture, which was properly understood in the West only after World War II. Yet as the 1920s came to an end, not much hope was left for the various Soviet avant-garde movements.

1932–1953

On April 23, 1932, a Communist Party decree with a matter-of-fact title, "Concerning the Restructuring of Literary-Artistic Organizations," effectively issued a death sentence to the entire Russian avant-garde. The document demanded a disbanding of all creative groups, and their reunification under the banner of centralized artistic unions controlled by the Party apparatus.

The reasons for such a definite change of cultural course have been continually disputed. Official Soviet propaganda has long stated that the Russian people themselves rejected the formalism of avant-garde movements and demanded a different art and architecture: realistic, accessible, and inspiring. The Party, then, sensed the popular sentiment and sanctioned the change. "Yes, I held out my hand to the left artists, but the proletariat and the peasantry did not hold out theirs," stated Anatoly Lunacharsky, a head of the Commissariat of Education during the 1920s.[27] Architect Ivan Fomin speculated in 1934: "The poverty of [Constructivist] form did not correspond to the great development and mighty achievements of our socialist epoch. Soviet citizens and people's organizations require a bright, buoyant architecture, they need an environment that stimulates energetic, joyful, pleasant life."[28]

Western researchers have maintained that the enforced return to realistic styles had little to do with the people's will. They relate it to the totalitarian rule of the Soviet state in the early 1930s, when Stalin amassed tremendous political power for himself. These experts have compared socialist culture under Stalin with that of Germany under Hitler, Cuba under Castro, and China under Mao. Thus a universal pattern of "totalitarian art" has emerged, art that falls under complete control of the State and is forced to serve as an ideological weapon. According to this model, "From the

multiplicity of artistic movements then in existence, the State selects one movement, always the most conservative, which most nearly answers its needs and declares it to be official and obligatory."[29]

Lately it has been noted that in the 1930s, even Western democratic cultures such as France or America underwent stylistic changes surprisingly similar to those taking place in Russia; most significantly, the return to figurative art, to classical architecture and decoration, exemplified by Art Deco. The postmodernist return to tradition in the 1980s has been brought into the argument as an example of a cultural shift that resulted from no political pressure. The advocates of this apolitical view offer a cyclical model, with avant-gardes and traditional movements taking historical turns. There is little relationship between architectural form and the prevailing system of government, say these critics; rather a socio-cultural momentum, gathered as a sum of independent manifestations of artistic will, serves as a principal motivation for an historical shift. Thus, Boris Grois argues that in 1932 the Communist party articulated a style whose time had come anyway.[30]

Paradoxically, these interpretations do not contradict, but complement each other. As has been mentioned above, even in the heyday of the revolutionary avant-garde, the Constructivist activity was supported neither by industries, nor by the nascent Soviet consumers, nor by the leaders in the Communist government. The State based its aesthetic decisions on a canonization of Lenin's opinion that "art must penetrate with its deepest roots into the very heart of the broad working masses. It must be understandable to these masses and loved by them."[31] Socialist Realism thus became the basis for a new aesthetic mandate, even though genuine folk art is almost never wholly realistic. To a large degree, this happened because of the shrewd and forceful activity of separate artistic groups that pursued their undistinguished careers

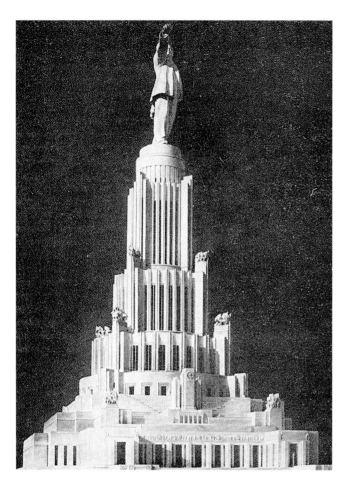

Above: Boris Iofan and others, *Palace of Soviets*, Moscow, 1932–56, model for 1934 scheme.

with the support of heavy Communist rhetoric. In painting, this was the stand of AKhRR group, heirs of the pictorial realists of the nineteenth century. In architecture, a group called the Organization of Proletarian Architects (VOPRA) took a position as the only ideologically correct movement in that field, accusing all others of subversion and bourgeois formalism. The monumental forms of their building projects only hinted at certain forthcoming architectural ideals.

Many professionals sincerely welcomed the new cultural climate, especially those of the younger generation, who were educated entirely in the Constructivist idiom of design. According to historian Selim Khan-Magomedov, "Many young [Russian] architects, who first encountered Classicism after they had completed their architectural training, saw it as something that was novel and full of unlimited creative potential."[32] However, most of the great masters of the Russian avant-garde—Tatlin, Melnikov, Leonidov, and Alexandr Vesnin—disagreed with the party line. The totalitarian state, as Hannah Arendt has noted, operates through ideology, organization, and terror, and it was the last two factors that effectively prevented the non-conformist architects from any substantial building activity. Some, including Constructivist leader Alexei Gan, were arrested and died in the labor camps. Russian culture was being dealt a heavy blow, the reverberations of which could be felt for generations to come.

The prevailing architectural ideology of the new direction was made public in 1932, in a brief for the competition to design the Palace of Soviets. For the first time, the government addressed the issue of style, requiring the entrants to draw on "the best examples of classical architecture." The brief "was a document of the State leadership, where the position of guidance over Soviet architecture had been clearly articulated," noted a contemporary observer.[33] The new, mandatory working method for all Soviet culture was defined by the Stalinist government as Socialist Realism. Its major tenets were unequivocally presented to prominent architects on a special private summons to the Kremlin,[34] and the charter of the newly established Union of Soviet Architects made them into the established norm. Soon they materialized in actual professional practice. The definition of Socialist Realism—"a combination of progressive Communist ideology with the realism of architectural image"[35]—sounds as cryptic today as it did to critically thinking architects in the early thirties. What constituted realism in architecture? Clearly, it did not include the avant-garde, but neither did it signify a mere return to the neoclassical forms of the nineteenth century. Architect Moisei Ginzburg, for instance, could not come to grips with the new directions: "They say: both adepts of classicism and modern Constructivists are equally alien to us. When they add that eclecticism is alien as well, one thinks it is simply a regulation against everybody."[36] Ginzburg tried to analyze Socialist Realism with logic alone, whereas the understanding of it required blind faith and devotion. This emotional factor was crucial, and most architectural definitions of the time inevitably incorporated it. "The necessary condition of this style is . . . the artist's loyalty to his country and his people," wrote Noi Trotsky, an architect of the time, who unwittingly captured Socialist Realism's very essence.[37]

Stylistically, socialist architecture demanded borrowings from all cultures simultaneously: not only

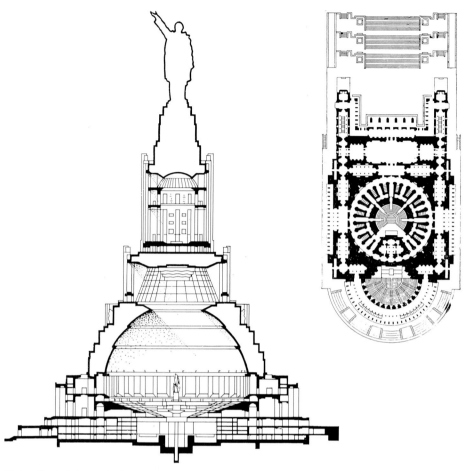

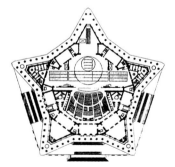

Above: Boris Iofan and others,
Palace of the Soviets, Moscow,
1932–56, section and plan for
1945 scheme.

Below and right: Karo Alabyan,
Theater of the Red Army, Moscow,
1934–40, exterior view and plan.

from the Greco-Roman classical tradition, but also from the Gothic, Muslim, Chinese, and Indian styles, and especially from the building vernacular of various national republics of the USSR. This heritage had to be handled with care, not juxtaposed freely (that was condemned as eclecticism), but reworked into a particular architectural synthesis. Architect Boris Iofan, for example, was praised because it was said he "knew how to fuse a lot of heterogeneous motifs into something organic and whole."[38] Iofan was chosen as one of the architects for the central structure of the Stalinist epoch, the Palace of Soviets, which started as a competition in 1932 and was never completed. (Group authorship of design under a close scrutiny by the Party leadership came to characterize the working process on large architectural commissions.) The colossal 1,360-foot-high palace was to stand taller than the Empire State Building. The entire pyramidal structure was to serve as a pedestal for a 330-foot statue of Lenin. All the aesthetic characteristics of socialist architecture found reflection in this legendary project: grandiose monumentality, verticalism, and the metaphorical verbalization of the architectural image.

Construction of the Moscow Metro was another major project undertaken in those years. From the outset, the Soviet architects on the job were instructed to create "the best underground in the world," a powerful symbolic monument, the successful completion of which in 1935 was compared to "the triumph of Socialism."[39] Far from being a utilitarian transportation system, the Moscow metro presented a series of marble-clad palatial stations, where "the great slogans of the socialist period were translated into the language of architecture." The ideological theme of each station penetrated all elements of its design, from the monumental mosaics to seating, signage, and ventilation grills. Perhaps the most spectacular example of Stalinist architecture, the underground achieved an unsurpassed degree of

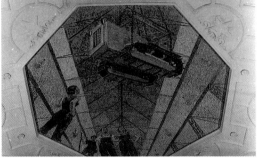

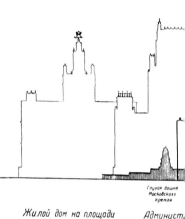

Top: Alexei Dushkin, *Revolution Square Station*, Moscow Metro, Second Line, 1938.

Center: Alexander Deineka, *Novokuznetskaya Station*, Moscow Metro, Third Line, 1944, ceiling mosaic.

Above: Alexei Dushkin, *Mayakovskaya Station*, Moscow Metro, Second Line, 1938.

integration between the built form and the verbal contents of propaganda.

The truisms of Socialist Realism had little meaning for industrial design in the Stalinist Soviet Union. In the absence of market competition, innovative design was unnecessary. Internal trade consisted of the distribution of generic basic goods, and foreign trade hardly existed. Ideologically, the concepts of function and usefulness, essential for any design production, were deeply alien to the Socialist culture. "The very idea of functionalism is bourgeois, as it expresses callousness of the capitalist industrial monopoly," wrote a leading critic in 1932.[40] Thus, the only thing criticized in the highly regarded Moscow Metro was the design of the subway cars, which were condemned for the "erratic glitter of their chrome tubing, the unpleasant paint of their doors, the casual shapes of lighting equipment which do not

harmonize with the joyful, beautiful architecture of the stations." "It would be ideal for the culture," concluded Vladimir Paperny, "if the subway car could grow out of the marble wall, and be itself marble-clad."[41] In fact, a lot of furniture and lighting for public interiors was designed in just this way: built-in, heavy, made of bronze and stone, and adorned with symbolic decoration.

Graphic design of the period also returned to traditional means. Rodchenko and Klucis still used elements of photomontage during the 1930s in a series of propaganda posters—haunting mixtures of Constructivist compositional techniques with a naturalistic depiction of the military regime. By the end of the decade, however, Klucis was arrested, and Rodchenko had switched exclusively to photography. Socialist Realism ruled the field, affecting both the form and content of printed production. In this

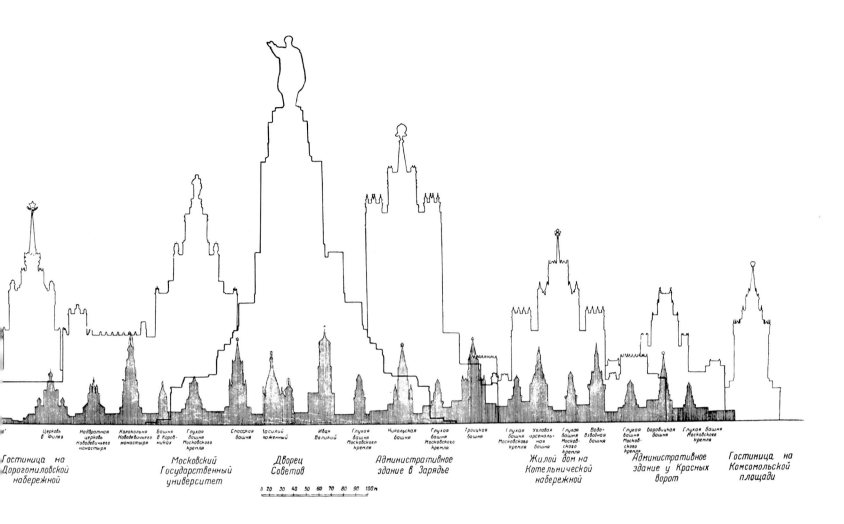

Above: Dmitry Chechulin and others,
High-rise building on Kotelnicheskaya,
Moscow, 1948–51.

manner, book design eventually took a secondary position to illustration, with easel artists taking leading positions in all areas of the graphic arts.

In 1945, after nearly four years of fighting the Nazi invasion, the Soviet Union emerged as a victorious nation in World War II. Stalinist culture, once nearly broken, reasserted itself in the rebuilding of destroyed Russian cities. Typically, it was not housing but government buildings, monuments, and promenades that became the focus of this reconstruction. The architectural goals for these gigantic urban projects, made possible by the free availability of the state-owned land, were straightforward: "To enlarge, to straighten, to decorate," as Vigdaria Khazanova noted.[42] Even though Moscow suffered less than other Russian cities in the war, for symbolic reasons it was the first on the list of government reclamation works. Eight high-rise buildings were planned for key

Moscow sites, designed to "change the entire image of the capital," and to signify "the beginning of a superior period of Socialist architecture"[43]—one combining modern techniques and materials with mythology of Socialist Realism. Seven of these stand today in Moscow, all of them approximations of the unbuilt Palace of Soviets, to which (it was specified) the high-rises had to be tied compositionally and thematically. A government directive specifically ordered the architects not to repeat the forms of American skyscrapers, which they decried as "gloomy heavy boxes that steal sun and air from the people."[44] The growing Cold War had begun, causing further cultural isolation for the entire Soviet society.

At the same time, Soviet industry received a significant technological boost from the West in the form of spoils of war. Whole factories were dismantled in Germany and moved to Russia, to be rebuilt for the manufacturing of consumer products and items of technology. The "design" of postwar Soviet cars, cameras, radios, and other items can be clearly traced to captured German products.[45] The streamlined automobile *Pobeda* (Victory) of 1946, whose innovative design remained unmatched in later Russian models, probably originated in Germany. In 1946, a project bureau was set up at the Ministry of Transportation to develop modifications of buses, railroad cars, and other vehicles. The automobiles, trams, and other means of transportation developed at the time remained a familiar feature in Soviet cities well into the 1970s.

1953–1985

By the time Stalin died on March 5, 1953, the situation in Soviet architecture was approaching threatening dimensions. Enormous funding had gone into the construction of monumental representative buildings (such as the seven Moscow high-rises), with nearly thirty percent of the total construction costs allocated to external facade decoration.[46] At the same time, most of the city population shared communal apartments, where each person was entitled to forty square feet of living space. Virtually all people in the countryside lived in cabins without running water or sewage systems, and even electricity was not widespread.

In 1954, the Congress of Builders, Architects, and Representatives of Industrial Ministries took place in the Kremlin. There, new Communist Party leader Nikita Khrushchev condemned the practice of "architectural excesses" in construction and planning. As had been the case twenty years earlier, architects had to take a stand of public repentance. Alexander Vlasov, a chief architect of Moscow who produced dozens of over-decorated buildings during the previous decades, wrote in 1960, "Extravagances and industrialization can not coexist in a building. Columns, porticoes, and other accessories of academic heritage must not be hanged over a modern construction."[47] A popular comedy "A Million for a Smile" ridiculed architects for wasting fortunes of the State money on pathetic building decoration.

The Congress determined that individualized project activity should be replaced by standardized construction, based on a few prototypical designs. Declared Khrushchev, "We should find a limited number of model houses, schools, hospitals, kindergartens, nurseries, stores, and other buildings, and begin mass construction only in accord with planned models."[48] In reality, the government took two different routes: standardized building for the masses and special architecture for certain representative structures. Such

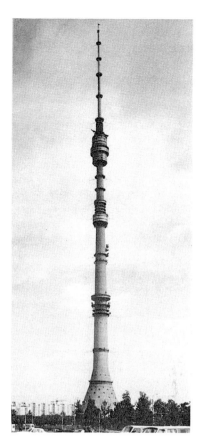

Above: Nikolai Nikitin and Leonid Batalov, *Television Tower*, Ostankino, 1960–67.

duality was characteristic of Khrushchev's politics, where pragmatism mixed easily with ideological conservatism. "In the questions of art," Khrushchev was quoted as saying, "I am a Stalinist."[49] He personally oversaw the hounding of an emerging generation of progressive artists, poets, and writers, calling them "faggots, traitors, and agents of imperialism."[50] Not surprisingly, the representative architecture of this period, though more restrained with regard to detail, in spirit differed little from the Stalinist model. In any case, Socialist Realism remained a reigning aesthetic category for all creative arts, and its application was strictly enforced.

Nonetheless, young architects who had survived a harsh wartime childhood attempted to generate bold, new urban schemes, such as the NER (New Elements of Settlement) project. Published in 1966 by a group of Moscow architects (Alexei Gutnov, Ilya Lezhava, Zoe Kharitonova, and others), the project called for a new system of population resettlement, consisting of integrated residential elements. Each element was to have a spiral structure, suggesting limitless growth.

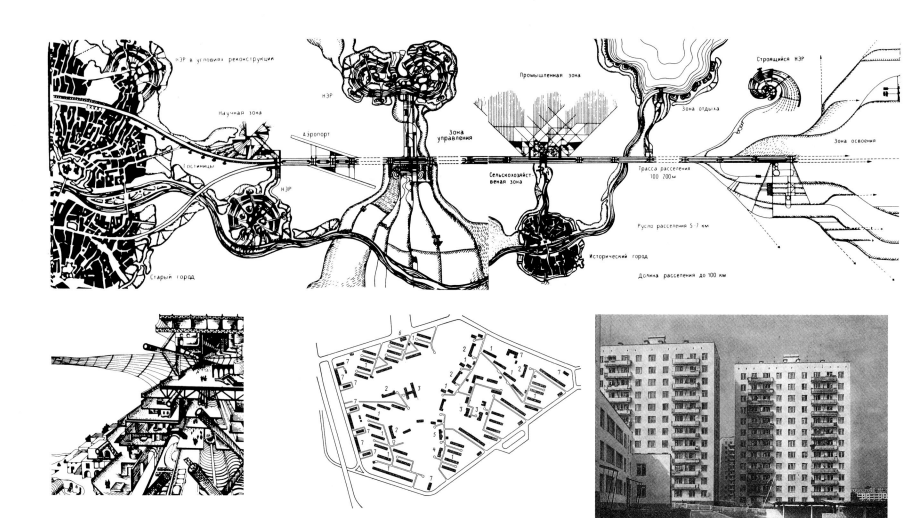

Top and above, left: NER Group,
New Elements of Settlement,
Moscow, 1966, master plan and
section of residential structure.

Above, center and right:
L. Golubovsky, A. Korabelnikov,
and others, *Micro-district #95 in
Kuntsevo*, Moscow, 1960s, master
plan and exterior view.

Providing essential living and recreational accommodations for thousands of people, it would also plug into a network of roads and green parks.[51] The initiative of the NER group was acknowledged by the government: its members were offered prestigious jobs and were even invited to the Kremlin. Yet their plan for a future Soviet architecture was never put into effect.

Instead, an industrial approach to mass-produced apartment houses resulted in the development of the most economical building type: a five-story, walk-up, ferro-concrete block of slab construction. This model, with few modifications, was built by the thousands on the periphery of every Soviet city in the form of micro-districts. There, these standardized blocks were scattered freely around a nucleus intended to house low buildings with shops and services; the construction of the latter was often delayed for years. This

approach alleviated somewhat the housing crisis, but the dreary micro-districts could hardly pass for "an architecture of the communist future." In 1969 a critical Communist Party resolution stated, "Methods of construction, residential planning decisions, and the external appearances of residences have become stereotyped. The architecture in areas of mass residential construction is dull and unattractive"—yet no substantial improvements took place on a mass scale.[52] Nicknamed "Khrushchev-slums" after the mastermind of this planning enterprise, the ubiquitous tenement blocks became an all-too-familiar sight for millions of people, a bleak and long-lasting symbol of post-Stalinist culture.

In the early 1960s some decisive steps were taken to introduce industrial design into the system of the Soviet economy. This decision was dictated by economic calculations rather than by any kind of

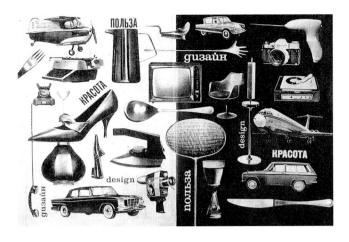

Above: Endpaper from *Krasota i Polza*, by Karl Kantor, the first Soviet book on design, published in 1967.

cultural philanthropy. An ever-larger quantity of goods was produced by Soviet industries; in 1963 a consumer could buy three times as many products as in 1950.[53] The wider choice of merchandise caused a serious overstock of inferior goods, impeding the state-run economy. Foreign trade also became an important factor in Soviet economic development, particularly among the Eastern Bloc countries. However, antiquated wares from the USSR did not sell abroad, and at home were shown up by relatively superior East German or Hungarian products. "As we enter the world market, where we must compete even with the developed capitalist nations, it is paramount that the quality of Soviet machines, tools, equipment—of all production—is not only at the level of the foreign output, but even better," declared Leonid Brezhnev, the Communist Party leader who succeeded Khrushchev in 1964.[54]

As the result of a special Party resolution regarding the improvement of product quality, the All-Union Research Institute of Technical Esthetics (VNIITE) was established in 1962 in Moscow. Soon the institute had branches in Leningrad and other major cities, along with a few design bureaus at key industrial sites. Curiously, the word "design" was relegated to Western practice, and therefore rarely used by Soviet bureaucrats. Cumbersome terms like "artistic engineering" or "technical aesthetics" were employed to emphasize the unique nature of design in the Soviet Union. Attempts to apply the principles of Socialist Realism to the field of design resulted in a confused, idealistic rhetoric. "Today a Western designer makes industrial products that improve the comfort of philistine life. But a Soviet constructor has to create an environment that does not relax a person, does not cause an atrophy of his physics, but instead,

stimulates his comprehensive and harmonious development," claimed the first Soviet book on design, published in 1967.[55] The practical methodologies of the capitalist world were not rejected—in fact, the dissemination of Western technical information and design magazines was encouraged at specialized professional libraries—yet foreign experience had to be corrected to achieve the utopian goal of "harmonizing human relationships through production." The newly established VNIITE was to take a leadership role in performing this illusory task.

VNIITE was organized with the active participation of Yuri Soloviev, who remained its director for more than twenty years. A functionary from the top levels of the Communist Party elite, he had enough connections to provide for the continuing government support of the institute.[56] As a subsidiary of the Ministry of Science and Technology, VNIITE became a scholarly organization, where theorists, historians, and even philosophers carried on research that had little connection with the country's economic reality. Instead of working directly with the industries in creating and improving products for the market, the institute was involved with large-scale integrated design programs, sometimes very advanced, and almost always unrealizable.

However, in its first years VNIITE enjoyed a brief period of energy and optimism. Many of the young professionals employed there genuinely believed they could make a difference, and hoped that a focused design effort could improve the quality of Soviet life. VNIITE proudly exhibited the best examples of these designs abroad, at foreign conferences and exhibitions. An important event took place in 1975, when VNIITE hosted the Ninth Annual ICSID (International Council of Societies of Industrial Design) Congress in Moscow. An inspired group of young designers worked for more than a year creating an environmental and graphic presentation for the

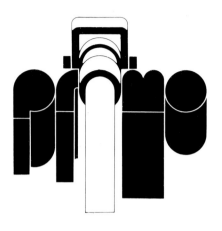

ELTEMEK

congress. Their display suggested a bold and effective concept of "poor design" comparable to the *arte povera* movement in Italy. Through bold graphics, corrugated cardboard furniture, and multi-screen projections, the group placed emphasis on raw creativity that made no attempt to compete with Western technological advances. This radical program looked politically suspicious to VNIITE authorities, and most of the display was shelved shortly before the first guests arrived in Moscow. In the course of the following years, the institute's most talented designers were forced to leave VNIITE to pursue their own creative paths on the margins of the design establishment.

Another branch of Soviet design developed under the patronage of the powerful State Union of the Artists. In 1965, a Central Experimental Studio was established at the Union, as a means of improving the quality of Soviet decorative arts. The head of the Studio, Evgeny Rosenblum, assisted by Mark Konik, established an unusual program that became very popular among designers. Twice a year the Studio

held seminars at the Senezh artists' colony, where the group worked on projects of industrial and environmental design. Rosenblum's Studio developed an alternative design philosophy and project methodology. Whereas professionals at VNIITE considered design a science, the Senezh group thought of it as art; they even called themselves "easel designers." Never preoccupied with the realization of their projects, they valued original concepts and state-of-the-art paper models as the final product of their creative activity. The Tower of Vladimir Tatlin, they argued, was an *unrealized* project of the Russian avant-garde, yet it exerted a paramount influence on all designers. Similarly, the Senezh group sought to influence 1970s design and architecture by introducing new ideas through exhibitions, discussions, and publications of their work.

Nevertheless, by the mid-1970s it was clear that design as a discipline remained unclaimed by the country's economic system. Industries did not want to employ designers, and wherever a designer stayed on staff, he or she was completely subordinate to the

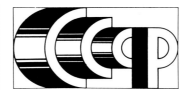

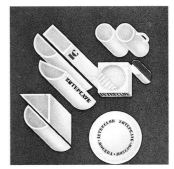

Above: Valery Akopov and Vasily Dyakonov, Logos for "Metal Industry of the USSR" exhibition, 1984.

Right: Boris Mikhailov, Tableware designed for use by athletes and members of the press, Moscow Olympic Games, 1980.

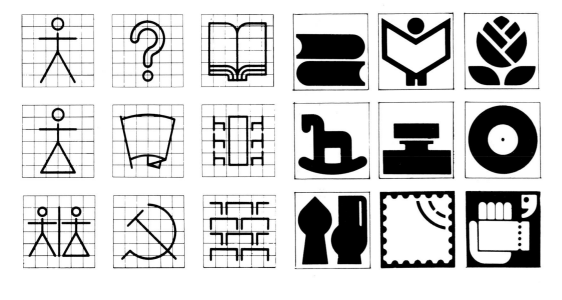

Above: Ramiz Guseinov, Signage program for the Electromera firm, 1980.

Above right: Pictogram system designed for the 1980 Moscow Olympics.

plant's director, engineer, and financial planner. Although VNIITE produced elaborate programs and prototypes, all well presented at professional exhibitions, the factories followed their own strategy. Foreign samples were routinely purchased at trade shows, dismantled, and copied, usually with gross simplifications. Shortages and irregular distribution of goods forced these unappealing products on the mass consumer.

Since the 1960s, graphic design has become an integral part of the attempted design revival in the USSR. A separate studio at VNIITE, as well as the Studio Promgraphika of the State Art Foundation, were the centers of this new initiative. Greatly influenced by the functional style of Swiss graphics, Soviet designers wanted to produce a coherent system of visual communication as a means of bringing order into a chaotic environment. "It seemed to us that graphic design had mastered an absolute, timeless methodology, and had its expression in a particular, modular, minimalist style,"[57] wrote Elena Chernevich. According to design critic Sergey Serov, this method

was characterized by a "diffused quality." Functionalist elements were mixed with the remnants of Socialist Realism, as in a series of pictograms for the Moscow Olympic Games of 1980. Like their colleagues in industrial design, Soviet graphic artists were mostly involved in large-scale visual identity programs for ministries and export firms. Everyday items of graphic design, such as packaging, periodicals, and urban signage, as a rule stayed unaffected by those "super-tasks, super-projects, and super-programs."[58]

The long period of Leonid Brezhnev's leadership of the country (1964–82) has been dubbed "the years of stagnation." The economic and political direction of the government aimed at maintaining a status quo, disregarding threatening signs of malfunctions in the system. Culturally, it was a period of conservative attitudes and increased censorship. The years of stagnation also witnessed an exodus of young professionals from the established architectural and design organizations. Many tried to find a niche on the margins of the official professional system, where they could more easily avoid political and artistic conformity in pursuit of their creative interests.[59] Exhibition design, teaching at alternative studios, production of posters for movies and theater—these are just a few occupations that former architects and industrial designers assumed during this period. Not incidentally, the most interesting and challenging design work was produced on the creative margins. "It seemed that the gripped groan of the country, the political dumbness, had been sublimated into solitary breakthroughs in art," recalled poet Andrei Voznesensky.[60] The defiant works of this period have formed, to a large degree, the contents of this book.

Perhaps the brightest manifestation of self-generated creativity was the phenomenon of Paper Architecture. It started in 1981, when a few young architects in Moscow tried to enter the annual international com-

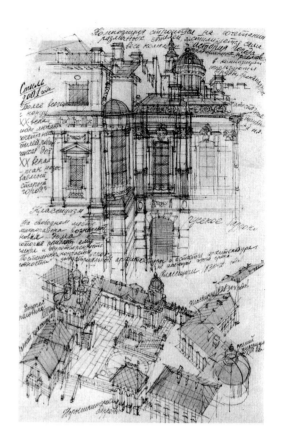

petition of a Japanese architectural magazine—one of the few such contests that did not require a prohibitive (hard currency) entry fee. To the amazement of the jurors and the participants themselves, several of the top prize winners were Russian (Michael Belov, Alexander Brodsky and Ilya Utkin, Michael Filippov and Nadia Bronzova). Soon hundreds of young architects and students around the country followed this lead, and the Paper Architecture movement was born. In 1984 these works were first exhibited in Moscow and received a mixed reaction, including some harsh criticism. The name of the group alluded to a derogatory label affixed to the utopian ideas of the Constructivists, who were frequently accused of creating "paper architecture" during their persecution in the 1930s. "The greatest sin of our modern architecture was that it had been mostly on paper, and this paper had been completely divorced from real practice," said a repentant Victor Vesnin in 1934.[61] The young architects, however, consciously took a polemical stance, emphasizing their lack of interest in construction, conventional practice, and the structure of the architectural establishment. The

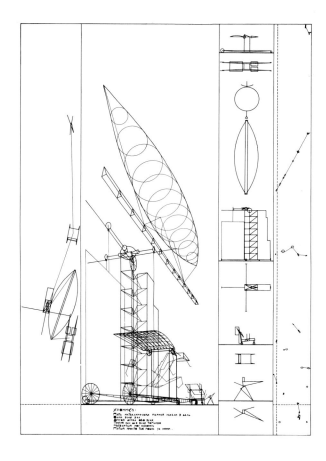

Above, top and bottom: Dmitry Velichkin, Paper Architecture, 1986.

Above right: Yuri Kuzin, *Sources of Urban Energy*, 1988, project.

Union of Soviet Architects decided after deliberations "that international recognition [for Paper Architecture] was advantageous to the State and that the initiative should not be suppressed."[62]

Meticulously drawn during long nights and weekends, the stunning drawings of Paper Architecture represent an architectural vision of a complex imaginary city, full of narratives, cultural allegories, and diverse styles and languages. The culture of Socialist Realism and its unsightly architectural manifestation—standardized micro-districts of concrete tenement blocks—conditioned this nostalgic, poetic outlook. Yet the designs rarely offer any tangible solutions for urban improvement; they are in the words of the Paper Architects' mentor Ilya Lezhava, "projects of projects," a constant laboratory for architectural research.[63] The constructivist experiments of

El Lissitzky or Chernikhov may appear spiritually close to the aim of Paper Architecture, yet the difference between the earlier Russian avant-garde and the recent conceptualism is fundamental. "It is no longer utopia, but fantasy," writes Alexander Rappaport. "Fantasy proposes a possible, but not obligatory or normative scheme. The standpoint of the author is relative, reflective, admits other approaches and sometimes looks ironically at the work's own methods."[64] The young architects view their projects as personalized, highly subjective options to the existing state of things. No manifesto of Paper Architecture has ever been written. Born on the margins of a profession during the years of stagnation, Paper Architecture has remained a commentary.

1985–1991

The first years of Mikhail Gorbachev's reform program promised to be a golden age for Soviet design. In 1986, a year after his appointment as the Communist Party leader, Gorbachev initiated a three-part program of economic revival: perestroika (restructuring), glasnost (public openness), and democratization. Generated at the top, the reform originally intended to preserve the Soviet regime intact, but to make it more productive and perhaps more human. Again, as in the early sixties, industrial design was perceived as a necessary, yet under-utilized economic tool. During his visit to a giant automobile plant, Gorbachev spoke out, demanding good design from car makers, as well as from the rest of the Soviet industry. His use of the word "design" (instead of the familiar term "artistic engineering") was so unusual that some newspapers even omitted it from their reports. Far from being a slip of the tongue, Gorbachev's call effectually indicated a new Party directive aimed at boosting industrial design.

In April 1987, a constituent congress of the Society of Soviet Designers took place at VNIITE in Moscow. Strange meeting it was, as no one knew who had qualified to be a member, or who had a right to accept or reject new candidates for membership. Eventually, everybody present was admitted, with the ubiquitous Yuri Soloviev elected as a president. In addition to industrial designers, the Society included interior architects, graphic artists, and even fashion stylists. As the first private enterprises, or cooperatives, were legalized, designers were encouraged to open private studios, where they could work on a contract basis with the factories. The words of the Deputy Prime Minister were widely quoted: "There is a need for design everywhere, and our industry is ready to shower the designers with commissions. Now it's up to you!"[65]

Unfortunately, events took a different course. An unplanned side-effect of Gorbachev's reforms manifested itself in political and national instability that spread throughout the different regions of the country. This last blow to the centralized bureaucratic system threw the Soviet Union into a deep economic crisis, the most visible characteristics of which have become inflation and perennial shortages. Lack of the most elementary goods and supplies, in particular, has nullified any serious design effort. In direct contrast to a capitalist economy, where a competitive market constantly dictates the introduction of new and superior products, the empty stores in Russia cry out for any merchandise, whether new or old, well-designed or unattractive. It was hoped that private enterprises would provide the necessary competition to spur creativity. Alas, a profiteering mentality and flea-market aesthetic dominated most cooperatives, making them an unlikely venue for the designers' talents. A private Moscow restaurant called Atrium, lovingly designed and constructed by Paper Architecture protagonists Alexander Brodsky, Ilya Utkin, and Eugeny Monakhov in 1988, has remained a singular exception.

Some designers are eager to join the new class of entrepreneurs, forming ventures with cooperatives,

factories, and export firms. Perhaps this is the last chapter of the familiar exodus from the design profession that started back in the 1970s. Instead of providing creative impetus, however, this transformation threatens to culminate in a mercantile, profit-oriented position. For instance, architect Maxim Poleschuk formed a joint venture with an aviation plant and a glass factory. They set about producing conference and coffee tables, fashioned from thick aviation glass. The prototypes, reminiscent of low-end commercial Italian production, indicate the direction of their product line. Poleschuk acknowledges the ambiguity of being a designer-cum-businessman in the conditions of an indiscriminate Soviet market.

By 1990, government planning and control over the industrial sector had virtually come to an end, even though the State formally retained ownership of property. In October 1990, leading Soviet design theorists and practitioners published an open letter in which they delineated the threatening situation in the design field: "If previously design was introduced into the economy by means of pushing and nagging, resolutions and directives, now there is a complete vacuum. Nobody wants to spend resources on design research. 'Who cares about aesthetics!'—this is the motto of today's industrialist." The writers of the letter addressed government leaders and private industrialists, desperately trying to prove the usefulness of their profession: "The unclaimed talent of a designer, his or her unwanted knowledge, is more than somebody's private misfortune. It is a strategic mistake with serious economic and cultural consequences."[66]

The predicament of design relates to a wider process of "cultural commodification" that has already affected Soviet theater, cinema, and literature. Market considerations, often vulgar and shortsighted, are being applied to all kinds of artistic endeavors to judge their viability. As the well-known iconoclastic writer Andrei Bitov has put it bitterly, "'It is forbidden' has already been replaced by 'Why bother?'"[67]

Those who are unable or unwilling to emigrate and who reject professional compromises often find themselves at a strange creative impasse. Mark Konik, one of the leaders of the Senezh studio during the seventies, declined to participate in the 1989 studio show, offering the following commentary: "For twenty-five years I have been working on design transformations of the urban environment. *Now I refuse to design.* The basis of our environment is worthless in all senses: architecturally, ecologically, socially, and culturally. To propose any artistic improvements is simply immoral. One has to start from the beginning, from the basis."[68] There is a sad irony here, since for decades, projects of the Senezh studio have served precisely as an ethical counterpart to the official architectural mentality. As the ruling system withers away, progressive design accepts a new challenge, a different morality. Instead of supplying an alternative rhetoric, such design wants to take an active part in the actual transformation of the landscape, however impossible this task might appear in the 1990s. Perhaps for these reasons, the Paper Architecture movement has ceased to exist, "having lost its initial meaning as an alternative," explained one of its founders, Yuri Avvakumov.

A similar situation in graphic design has forced talented young graphic artists to abandon the conventional methodology of their discipline. Some, like Vladimir Chaika and Alexander Gelman, frustrated with "projects that nobody needs, that burst like soap bubbles at the touch with the Soviet reality," have in essence left the field, confining their work to a select group of client-friends.[69] They have

МЕМОРИЛ

sought to create a new style based on existing condition. Permutations of this trend have been variously described as a "poetry of refusal," an "aesthetics of poverty," or simply as "blackness." The motto of Alexander Ermolaev's studio TAF—"design for survival"—captures the sentiment behind this creative direction. The followers of "poor design" use cheap, readily available materials and employ foolproof compositional methods that cannot be ruined even by inferior Soviet workmanship. Crooked margins, uncoordinated type, and one- or two-color printing often serve both as an aesthetic expression and as the only technical solution for a given project. These rough works can lay claim to representing the graphic design of perestroika.

However, no single trend could describe the variety of artistic expression in the Russia of the 1990s. Pluralism has become a form of creative freedom after long years of a single state-established style. Indeed, in an off-shoot of glasnost and democratization, government control over culture has come to an end. It is tempting to connect the multifaceted variety of new Russian design to the postmodern condition, considering the new openness toward the West. But the former Soviet Union is far from the advanced knowledge- or technology-based position of postindustrial society. "We have not in any major way entered the information revolution," acknowledges leading Russian scientist Sergei Kapitza.[70]

A study by John Rajchman, however, shows that economic and political background have little to do with "the meaning the term postmodern has meanwhile acquired in actual artistic practice: that of style with an ideology."[71] Any style, as well as any ideology, can be imported, adopted, and even considered one's own, as Russia has proved more than once during its one-thousand-year-old history. The two most important moments in the growth of a truly Russian culture were an acceptance of Byzantine civilization at the outset, and an influx of Western values under Peter the Great. At the end of the nineteenth century, religious philosophers Soloviev and Fyodorov advocated the cosmic idea of the Russian soul as the providential kin of every nation on earth. The particular character of the Russian spirit has allowed for an organic merging of different cultural influences. Apparently, this never-ending process continues in the 1990s. "If McDonald's has come to Moscow, why not postmodernism?" asks W.J.T. Mitchell.[72] A new cultural context brings a

Above: Sergey Malakhov,
Apartment building, Samara, 1989,
model.

Left: Alexander Brodsky, Ilya Utkin,
and Evgeny Monakhov, *Atrium
restaurant*, Moscow, 1988,
interior. Photograph by Igor Palmin.

Right: Evgeny Monakhov, *Foot-
Scissors*, 1989, competition
project.

Below: Vladimir Zolotov, *Black-Red
Telephone*, 1987, prototype.

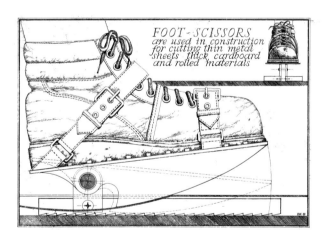

FOOT-SCISSORS
are used in construction
for cutting thin metal
sheets, thick cardboard
and rolled materials

special significance to this latest Western import. "Under these circumstances," observes Heinrich Klotz, "a neo-constructivist design in the style of Chernikhov or Leonidov, or even the colorful façade of a neo-Palladian villa, which in western eyes already seems obsolete in the sense of Postmodern, stereotyped historicism, presents itself as an act of liberation. [T]he tawdry embellishment turns into the justification for survival. The valve opens under this pressure and hisses down to the level of a softer calmness. This, too, is perestroika."[73]

Arata Isozaki has said: "I am an architect of the postmodern age, but not a postmodernist architect."[74] The protagonists of the new Russian design might claim exactly the opposite. Although the postmodern age never truly arrived to Russia, the designers eagerly and confidently absorbed the basic vocabulary of the movement. Eclecticism, irony, double reading, disregard of originality, and especially "the eclipse of all of the affect"[75] have come to characterize their prodigious body of work. "This is postmodernism, or in our case post-socialist-realism, filtered through one's own soul," wrote Sergey Serov. "It seems the work is completely yours, deeply personal; then it proves to be a sign of the times."[76]

NOTES

1. Karl Kantor, *Krasota i Polza* (Moscow: Iskusstvo, 1967): 154–174.

2. Anatolii Strigalev, "The Art of the Constructivists: From Exhibition to Exhibition, 1914–1932," *Art Into Life* (New York: Rizzoli, 1990): 17.

3. Igor Golomstock, *Totalitarian Art* (New York: Harper Collins, 1990): x.

4. Quoted from Christina Lodder, "Constructivism and Productivism in the 1920s," *Art Into Life* (New York: Rizzoli, 1990): 100. My rendering of Production Art here and further relies on this incisive text.

5. Lodder, *Art Into Life:* 100.

6. Lodder, *Art Into Life:* 102.

7. Strigalev, *Art Into Life:* 31.

8. Selim O. Khan-Magomedov, *Pioneers of Soviet Architecture* (New York: Rizzoli, 1987): 65.

9. Szymon Bojko, "Vkhutemas," *The Avant-garde in Russia, 1910–1930: New Perspectives* (Cambridge: The MIT Press, 1980): 78.

10. Bojko, *The Avant-garde in Russia:* 80.

11. Quoted from John Milner, *Vladimir Tatlin and the Russian Avant-garde* (New Haven and London: Yale University Press, 1983): 194.

12. Lodder, *Art Into Life:* 104.

13. N.D. Adaskina and D.V. Sarabianov, *L.S. Popova* (Moscow, State Tretyakov Gallery, 1990): 133.

14. Lodder, *Art Into Life:* 106.

15. Nina Lobanov-Rostovsky, "Revolutionary Ceramics," *American Ceramics* (9/2, 1991): 40–46.

16. Selim O. Khan-Magomedov, *Lazar Markovich Lissitzky 1890–1941* (Moscow: State Tretyakov Gallery, 1990): 38.

17. Vasilii Rakitin, "Gustav Klucis: Between the Non-Objective World and World Revolution," *The Avant-garde in Russia, 1910–1930: New Perspectives* (Cambridge: The MIT Press, 1980): 61–62.

18. Lodder, *Art Into Life:* 110.

19. Lodder, *Art Into Life:* 150.

20. Milner, *Vladimir Tatlin and the Russian Avant-garde:* 202–205.

21. Gail Harrison Roman, "The Ins and Outs of Russian Avant-Garde Books: A History, 1910–1932," *The Avant-Garde in Russia, 1910–1930: New Perspectives* (Cambridge: The MIT Press, 1980): 106–108.

22. V.V. Kirillov, *Put' Poiska I Experimenta* (Moscow: MGU Publishers, 1974): 46.

23. Kirillov, *Put' Poiska I Experimenta:* 47.

24. Anatole Senkevitch, Jr., "The Sources and Ideals of Constructivism in Soviet Architecture," *Art Into Life* (New York: Rizzoli, 1990): 185–186.

25. Senkevitch, *Art Into Life:* 183.

26. Khan-Magomedov, *Pioneers of Soviet Architecture:* 233.

27. Golomstock, *Totalitarian Art:* 29.

28. M.A. Minkus, *Fomin* (Moscow: Gos Izdatelstvo Literaturi Po Arkhitekture, 1953): 68. All Soviet publications until the late 1980s advocated the same position.

29. Golomstock, *Totalitarian Art:* xii.

30. Boris Grois, "Socialist Realism as Gestamkunstwerk," lecture at The Russian Avant-Garde Conference, Los Angeles, 1990. See also the book of Vladimir Paperny, *Kultura Dva* (Ann Arbor: Ardis, 1985).

31. Golomstock, *Totalitarian Art:* 174.

32. Khan-Magomedov, *Pioneers of Soviet Architecture:* 262.

33. M.A. Il'in, *Vesniny* (Moscow, Akademia Nayk SSSR, 1960): 105.

34. Il'in, *Vesniny:* 109–110. Architect Victor Vesnin who was one of the invited, described the event in an article, entitled "I will remember this for the rest of my life."

35. M.P. Tsapenko, *O Realisticheskih Osnovah Sovetskoi Arkhitekturi* (Moscow: Gos Izdatelstvo Literaturi Po Arkhitektury, 1952): 74.

36. Vladimir Paperny, *Kultura Dva* (Ann Arbor: Ardis, 1985): 28–29. This book, long overdue in English translation, remains the best source of information about Stalinist architecture.

37. Tsapenko, *O Realisticheskih:* 270.

38. I.U. Eigel, *Boris Iofan* (Moscow: Stroyizdat, 1978): 10.

39. See Constantin Boym, "La Città Ideale è Sottoterra," *Modo* (N. 88, April 1986): 46–49.

40. Quoted in Kantor, *Krasota i Polza:* 146.

41. Paperny, *Kultura Dva:* 216.

42. Vigdaria Khazanova, "Beretch Mechtatelei I Providtsev," *Arkhitectura i Sroitel'stvo Moskvi* (March, 1988): 6.

43. N.P. Bylinkin, *Vysotnye Zdania V Moskve* (Moscow: Gos Izdatelstvo Literatyri Po Arkhitecture, 1951): 5.

44. Bylinkin, *Vysotnye:* 8.

45. Reported by Vitaly Komar and Alex Melamid. Melamid's own uncle worked on such assignments in the late 1940s.

46. Igor Golomstock, "Union of Soviet Socialist Republics," *International Handbook of Contemporary Developments in Architecture,* Warren Sanderson, ed. (Westport and London: Greenwood Press, 1981): 489.

47. M.G. Barkhin, ed., *Mastera Sovetskoi Arkhitekturi Ob Arkhitekture* (Moscow: Iskusstvo, 1975): 515.

48. Golomstock, *International Handbook:* 490.

49. Andrei Voznesensky, *Aksioma Samoiska* (Moscow: IKPA, 1990): 330.

50. See memoirs of Andrei Voznesensky, Mikhail Romm, and the book by John Berger *Art and Revolution* (New York: Pantheon, 1969).

51. Anatole Kopp, *Town and Revolution* (New York, George Brazilier, 1970): 237.

52. Golomstock, *International Handbook:* 492.

53. Karl Kantor, *Voprosy Tekhnicheskoi Estetiki,* No. 2, (Moscow: Iskusstvo, 1970): 65.

54. Kantor, *Voprosy:* 79.

55. Kantor, *Krasota i Polza:* 194.

56. A common Western misunderstanding regarded Yuri Soloviev as a practicing designer, and prompted some prestigious European companies (Alessi, Thonet) to invite him for collaboration. In fact, as Government support for VNIITE nearly ended in 1990, Soloviev left the institution and abandoned any design activity.

57. Quoted from Sergey Serov, "Oglyadivayas' Na 80e," *Reklama* (No. 1, 1990): 12.

58. Serov, *Reklama* (No. 1, 1990): 13.

59. Constantin Boym, "Notes from the Underground," *ID* (May/June 1989): 29–31. In the article, I defined this phenomenon as "escape to design."

60. Voznesensky, *Aksioma Samoiska:* 314.

61. Il'in, *Vesniny:* 160.

62. Alexander Rappaport, "Language and Architecture of 'Post-Totalitarianism,'" *Paper Architecture: New Projects from the Soviet Union* (New York: Rizzoli, 1990): 11.

63. Ilya Lezhava, "Panorama Molodykh," *DI* (No. 12, 1987): 6.

64. Alexander Rappaport, "Fantasy Versus Utopia," *Nostalgia of Culture* (London: The Architectural Association, 1988): 9.

65. "Otkrytoe Pismo," *Tekhnicheskaya Estetika* (No. 10, 1990): 1.

66. "Otkrytoe Pismo": 1.

67. On the "commodification" of culture, see the article by Nancy Condee and Vladimir Padunov, "Makulakul'tura: Reprocessing Culture," *October* (No. 57, Summer 1991): 88.

68. Mark Konik, "Proectirovanie istchezaet," *DI* (No. 10, 1989): 2.

69. Serov, *Reclama* (No. 1, 1990): 13.

70. Sergei Kapitza, "Essay: The State of Soviet Science," *Scientific American* (June 1991): 132.

71. John Rajchman, "Postmodernism in a Nominalist Frame," *Flash Art,* (No. 137, 1987): 49–51.

72. W.J.T. Mitchell, "Framed in Moscow," *Boston Review* (June/August 1991): 13–14.

73. Heinrich Klotz, "Preface," *Paper Architecture: New Projects from the Soviet Union* (New York: Rizzoli, 1990): 7–8.

74. Lecture at the Domus Academy in Milan in June 1986.

75. Frederic Jameson, "Foreword" in Jean-Francois Lyotard, *The Postmodern Condition: A Report on Knowledge* (Minneapolis: University of Minnesota Press, 1984): xviii.

76. Sergey Serov, "Chaika Segodnya," *Reclama* (No. 5, 1990): 11.

NEW RUSSIAN DESIGN

Paper Architecture

Opposite: *Crystal Palace*, 1982, first prize in the Central Glass Company competition in Japan.

ALEXANDER BRODSKY and ILYA UTKIN

At the end of 1987, a special conference of architects and urban planners took place in the Russian capital. Its title—"Achievements and Losses in 70 years of Moscow Architecture"—was unprecedented for the Soviet professional establishment. For seventy years one was allowed to talk only of achievements; now, in the liberated atmosphere of glasnost, most speakers chose to concentrate on losses.

Many traced their disappointment to the General Plan of Moscow Reconstruction, signed into effect in 1935, which called for a massive rebuilding of the city. Although Old Moscow had an existing historical urban structure, the plan demanded that room for new construction be created. Starting in the 1930s, an avalanche of ruthless, often meaningless demolitions took place in the old city, as churches, city walls, and picturesque side-streets were replaced with fields of asphalt. Those few preservationists who raised their voices risked their careers and lives to do so. Massive architectural interventions continued to violate the city fabric in the postwar years of Stalinist triumph, again in the 1960s, and even in the late Brezhnev period, up to the time of perestroika. When in 1987 architects remembered things gone, they talked about the disappearance of the city's character, about the lost human scale of its buildings and streets, and especially about the dismantling of its once sophisticated urban culture.

Moscow architects Alexander Brodsky and Ilya Utkin expressed these very same feelings, years before

glasnost sanctioned the debate, in their first Paper Architecture projects. *Crystal Palace,* their winning entry in a 1982 competition hosted by a Japanese architectural magazine, was a projection of unfulfilled urban memories and desires. An accompanying text read, in part, "A person who wants to visit it will make his way through blocks of slums and dumps, but coming at last to the Palace will find neither roof nor walls—only huge glass plates stuck into a huge box of sand. A mirage remains simply a mirage, though it can be touched."

The personal memories of Brodsky and Utkin, from early childhood onward, have become inseparable from their architectural recollections of the city. Utkin is a third-generation architect. Brodsky's father, Savva, was a celebrated graphic artist who was awarded honorary membership at the Academy of Fine Arts in Madrid for his illustrations to *Don Quixote.* Both were born in 1955, and they met as students during their first semester at the Moscow Architectural Institute. They collaborated often during their school years, and upon graduation in 1978 were even given a single diploma with both their names on it. Having finished three obligatory years of internship, the friends became immersed in their own artistic-architectural projects, rendering them in their favored etching medium. They worked prodigiously at a loft-like studio, filled with books and paintings that Brodsky inherited from his late father.

Most of Brodsky and Utkin's graphic works are devoted to the city. Their concern regarding the lost cultural values of contemporary urban life has often been defined as nostalgia, a term that inevitably misses the transformative energy and inventiveness of their architectural ideas. *A Museum of Vanished Houses* proposes honoring the memory of demolished Moscow buildings, "regardless of whether, during their lifetime, they were architectural monuments," with scale models installed in the gridded wall of a

Crystal Palace is a beautiful but infeasible dream, a Mirage which calls you, always seen at the edge of visible. But as each dream in close examination it will prove the other thing than it seemed afar. A person, who wants to visit it, will make a long way through the town borderland, blocks of slums and dumps but coming at last to the Palace, find neither roof nor walls—only the huge glass plates, stuck into the huge box with sand. A Mirage remains simply a Mirage, though, it can be touched. Passing from one glass chink to another, a visitor will walk the Palace through and find himself at the border of a small square, where the Landscape commences. Did he learn the very essence of the Crystal Palace, will he have a desire to visit it once more? Nobody knows...

Crystal Palace

Sea-weed swarms with
Transparent fries. Catch them —
They shall thaw without a trace
Bashô

SECTION SCALE 1:666

Above: *Still Life* (detail), 1989.
Photograph by James Dee.

columbarium. A wrecking ball hangs from the ceiling as a sad reminder of destruction. "Each vanished house, even the most unprepossessing, is an equal exhibit in the museum. After all, each is suffused with the soul of its architect, builders, inhabitants, and even the passerby who happened to cast an absent-minded glance its way," they write. In this competition project, the poetics of preservation are inseparable from the humanist concern over the plight of an individual in the routine of solitary urban existence. Both the house *and* the passerby deserve a monument, a niche in Brodsky and Utkin's imaginary museum.

Solitude, as a theme, reappears in many of the duo's drawings, symbolized by a shadowy figure of a man with a hat and umbrella, rushing through streets or landscapes. In *Villa Nautilus* this man assumes tragic and grotesque overtones, worthy of one of Dostoevsky's heroes. He is equally lonely and defiant in his cellar, "in an absolutely closed and silent space," and in the middle of street traffic that rushes "in the mad pursuit of God knows what." The pathos of solitary estrangement is contrasted with the pleasure of friendly company in *A Ship of Fools*. The group that raises its glasses gathered atop a wooden skyscraper is modeled after Brodsky, Utkin, and their real-life friends, who performed a version of this merry ritual to help them survive the years of stagnation. The feast is raised way above the city streets, which provide a powerful backdrop, magnificent in their gloom and density.

This vision of city-as-spectacle influences and inspires many of Brodsky and Utkin's projects. "The life of a big city, perpetually changing, unpredictable and mysterious, is a theater for those who know how to appreciate it," write the authors. "He who opens the door to his house and goes out to buy some cigarettes is like a brave explorer who has ventured on a perilous journey. Millions of doors, leading God

knows where… Millions of windows, hiding God knows what… " The project for *A Stageless Theater* provides a tool for immersion in metropolitan mysteries: a truck with 198 seats and a small stage that moves about the city, stopping to provide a forum for casual and unexpected street scenes.

The humanism of Brodsky and Utkin's work becomes polemical in its distrust of technology. Everything, from the vernacular structures of their buildings to the old-fashioned truck of *A Stageless Theater* has the flavor of an antique shop. "A word in friendly conversation gives more than all the computers in the world," claim the architects in a project for "The Intelligent Market" competition. *Island of Stability*, an open-air museum of sculpture, is dedicated to "those who are tired of plastic vanity, who are sick of their foam rubber life." Accordingly, both designers would opt for the old values of Stalinist architecture over the faceless modernist idiom. "It was the age of the great builders," explains Brodsky. "After it, nobody could do such buildings. Nobody could make a column with a capital. Nobody could make good sculpture in architecture."

Brodsky and Utkin themselves tried the role of builders in 1989, when they worked on the Atrium restaurant in Moscow, in collaboration with their friend, architect Evgeny Monakhov. The restaurant is located on Leninsky Prospect, an enormously wide street swept through with penetrating winds. An entrance, a delicate portico, is attached to the facade of a huge housing block, as a charming and incongruous reminder of once-possible urban pleasures. Inside, there is an intricate dining hall, inspired by the courtyards of Italy: an exterior within an interior, filled with artificial light. Its manneristic, slightly distorted classical forms are very consistent with Brodsky and Utkin's graphic work. To achieve this, the architects crafted the entire interior themselves, forming and carving it out of stucco for

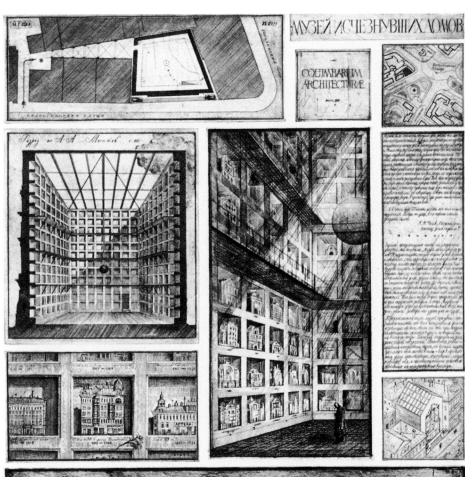

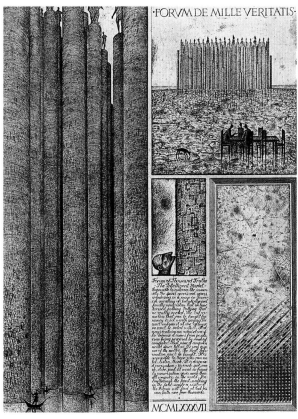

Above: *A Museum of Vanished Houses*, 1984, competition project, Moscow.

Right, top: *Villa Nautilus*, 1985, second prize in the Shinkenchiku competition in Japan.

Right, bottom: *Forum de Mille Veritatis*, 1987, honorable mention in "The Intelligent Market" competition in Japan.

Above: *Pedestrian bridge*, 1990, project for Tacoma, Washington.

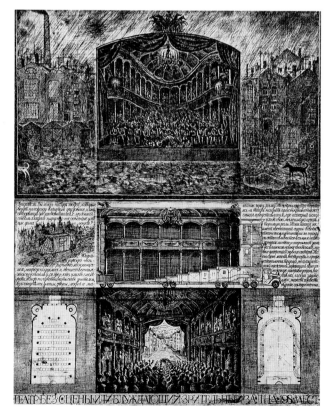

Left: *A Stageless Theater*, 1986, project for "A Theater and a City" competition, Moscow.

Opposite: *A Ship of Fools or A Wooden Skyscraper for the Jolly Company*, 1988, project for the Shinkenchiku competition in Japan.

five long months. In the opinion of Moscow architectural critic Evgeny Asse, the Atrium sets a new precedent for Russian architecture, bringing back a medieval, manual building tradition.

In 1990 Brodsky and Utkin got engaged in a much larger environmental project: a pedestrian bridge for the city of Tacoma, Washington. This project would be impossible to complete without a large building team and advanced construction technology, yet even here the architects reserved some details to be executed by their own hand. Spanning highways and railroad tracks, the bridge is planted with trees; seemingly leading nowhere, it becomes a place of contemplation, of rest, of momentary pause in the rush of contemporary life.

News of their competition awards and exhibitions abroad quickly established Brodsky and Utkin's reputation in the West. In spite of their architectural orientation, it was the art world that raised them into the roster of international stars, and turned their competition-entry etchings into precious commodities. Every year they spend less and less time in Moscow, being invited to take part in numerous art shows, festivals, and museum installations around the world. "Art, architecture: it's the same thing," retorted Utkin when questioned about a shift in orientation in the duo's work. In fact, their entire professional career has proven the profound truth of this thesis.

A Comfort in Metropolis

A Ship of Fools or a Wooden Sky-scraper for the Jolly Company·

41

Above and right: *Island of Stability*,
as installed at Ronald Feldman Fine
Arts gallery in New York, 1990.
Photographs by James Dee.

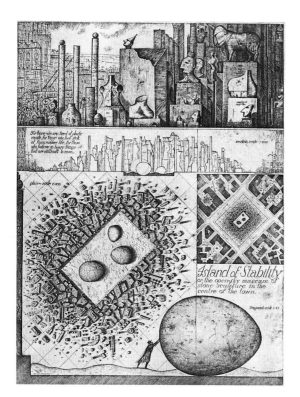

Above: *Island of Stability*, 1983,
entry in the Central Glass Company
competition in Japan, drawing.

Above and right, center: *Atrium restaurant*, 1988, Moscow (in collaboration with Evgeny Monakhov), views of the interior. Photographs by Igor Palmin.

Right, top and bottom: *Atrium restaurant*, lighting fixtures portraying the two architects.

MICHAEL BELOV

When an article by Michael Belov was published in a Soviet magazine in 1981, it started, appropriately for the times, with a quotation from the country's leader: "Our architecture needs deeper artistic expression and more diversity," stated Leonid Brezhnev at a Communist Party congress. This was hardly a revelation for the millions of people who inhabited tenement blocks throughout the country, from Moscow to Siberia.

Much of the nation's shoddy architecture was built in the sixties to ward off an acute housing crisis inherited from the Stalinist years. Large residential zones were planned at the peripheries of virtually every town, based on grossly simplified principles of Le Corbusier's "Radiant City." As with virtually every reform in Soviet society, good intentions ended up with disastrous results. The 1970s saw many attempts to humanize this monotonous and alienating environment, to diversify architectural character, to appeal to the *genius loci* of different areas and geographical regions. Yet the efforts of various architectural studios were largely wasted. A complex bureaucratic approvals process, unclear ideological guidelines regarding what exactly constituted socialist (versus capitalist) architecture, increasing self-censorship in the profession—all these brought forth more uniform, mediocre, repetitive buildings and town plans.

By the time Brezhnev had made his rhetorical statement, Michael Belov already knew how to make architecture different. Sometimes regarded as an architectural prodigy, he won his first international competition at twenty-one, while a junior at the Moscow Architectural Institute. In 1982, two years after his graduation, Belov was the first Russian to win a major prize in Japan's prestigious Shinkenchiku competition. The ambiguous brief for the competition called for a house that could also act as a museum of the twentieth century. Accordingly, Belov's house has a double identity: it provides a threatening and mysterious passage for the visitor, and an intricate and cozy home for the inhabitants. Our century is a deeply troubled and incomprehensible one, Belov seems to say, yet people manage to live in it, comfortably and joyfully. With its sophisticated plays on architectural scale, theatrical effects, and narrative content, the project established a future direction for Belov's work. Says the architect, "All my works begin with a scenario. Then, using all the graphic methods at my disposal, this scenario is brought to life on paper."

Although his formal and stylistic language fluctuate to suit a given project, and different styles are possible, Belov is usually recognized for his meticulous graphics, which are somewhat surrealist in spirit. This is evident in another Japanese competition project, *A Sculpture Museum,* which features a huge sculptural mask, half-buried inside a hill. Fragments of the portrait can be observed through peepholes set in the museum walls; the complete face, with its mirror-clad eyes, is open only to the sky. *The Intelligent Market,* a 1987 competition project, proposes a gathering of oracles as an alternative vision to the computerized society of the future. Belov writes, "Seven oracles below present ordinary information, three above present the important data, and one main oracle gives a final diagnosis." For a Soviet society long beset by demagogues, the project was both a pointed critique and a wistful fantasy of an electronic future.

In 1988, as the new economic policy of perestroika gave the green light to cooperative private enterprises, Michael Belov was one of the first to open his own architectural studio. Many international awards, years of teaching at Moscow Architectural Institute, and his

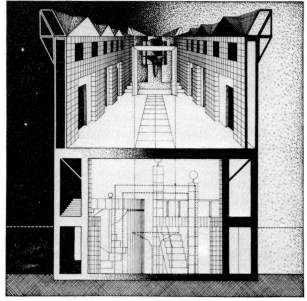

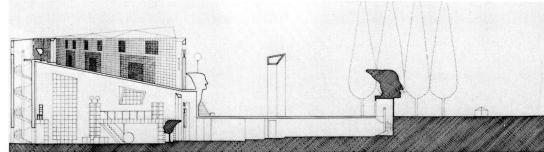

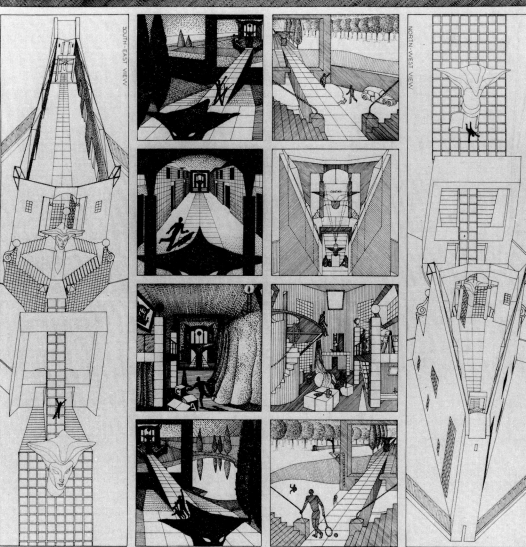

Above and right: *House/Museum of the Twentieth Century*, 1982, project, first prize in the Shinkenchiku Residential Design competition in Japan.

personal connections have given him considerable clout in professional circles. In less than ten years one could see his transformation from an energetic student into what foreign journalists variously describe as "a stocky Russian of insurpassable confidence," or "the ultimate bourgeois architect." He rented a studio space next door to the mansion of the Union of Soviet Architects, which gave his office, called Brigada A, an almost official character.

One of his first major projects has been Red Camp, a recreation complex near Moscow, on the picturesque banks of the Moskva River. A number of classical country estates decorated the landscape there in the nineteenth century; most of them were destroyed during the Revolution and in the proceeding years of mismanagement. Red Camp re-creates a familiar typology for the country estate: a porticoed main building, flanking wings, a gate, and decorative garden pavilions. Yet the structures are rendered at a much grander scale; the main building alone stands five stories high. The architectural treatment of the project utilizes canonical postmodernist "double coding": classical language is combined with modern construction materials and techniques. Belov advances this dichotomy even further in a project for a summer camp, called *Lutchik,* commissioned by the Ministry of Material Supplies. He describes his intent as "rotonda-mania," a long-cherished desire to re-create the renaissance forms of Palladio's Villa Rotonda on Russian soil. His project provides for no less than six identical rotonda-like buildings, all painted bright red, as children's sleeping quarters.

Curiously enough, in the same year Belov designed a building for the Cultural Initiative Foundation in Moscow that relies heavily on the idiom of Russian Constructivism. Such an eclectic choice of references seems problematic for many of Belov's critics, both in his homeland and abroad. Perhaps this could be interpreted as a sign of freedom after many years of tightly controlled socialist architecture. "I am the most famous living Russian architect," states Belov, "and I express myself any way I want." He himself points to Konstantin Melnikov, a maverick architect of the early Russian avant-garde, who also felt unconstrained by any single stylistic movement of his time. Historian Frederik Starr has called this great and original master of architectural form "a solo architect in a mass society." While never renouncing strict functionalism, Melnikov approached every project as a research into new possibilities for generating form. Thus, Melnikov described his Workers' Clubs, designed for several Moscow districts, as "the seven musical keys of a scale—seven different architectural themes."

Melnikov's famous motto—"Creativity begins at the point where one can say, 'This is mine'"—suggests an important difference between the master's architectural freedom and the liberties of Michael Belov. For Belov, the search for a new *image* replaces the discovery of new forms. For a recent project, a store interior in Moscow, he appropriated still another language—that of architectural rationalism. White gridded display elements recur throughout the interior, along with round columns, stripped of any decoration, and triangular beams with concealed lighting. Curiously, the very concept of a rationalist architectural grid seems to be defeated by the certainty of inferior workmanship in the execution of the design. Yet Belov believes it unreasonable, even immoral, to expect or to demand a Western-class construction quality from an impoverished and unprepared building industry. "Besides, it is not going to show up in the photographs," he sincerely adds. After years of working on paper, for him the photographs of a project are paramount; image value is equal to architectural quality.

Left: *Red Camp*, 1988, project for a recreational complex on Moskva River (in collaboration with Brigada A), conceptual site plan.

Below: *Red Camp*, facade of the main building.

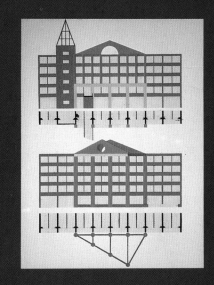

Near right and far right: Details of the *Red Camp* project.

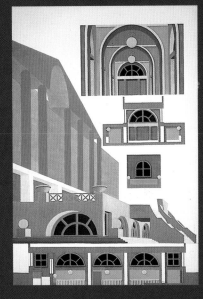

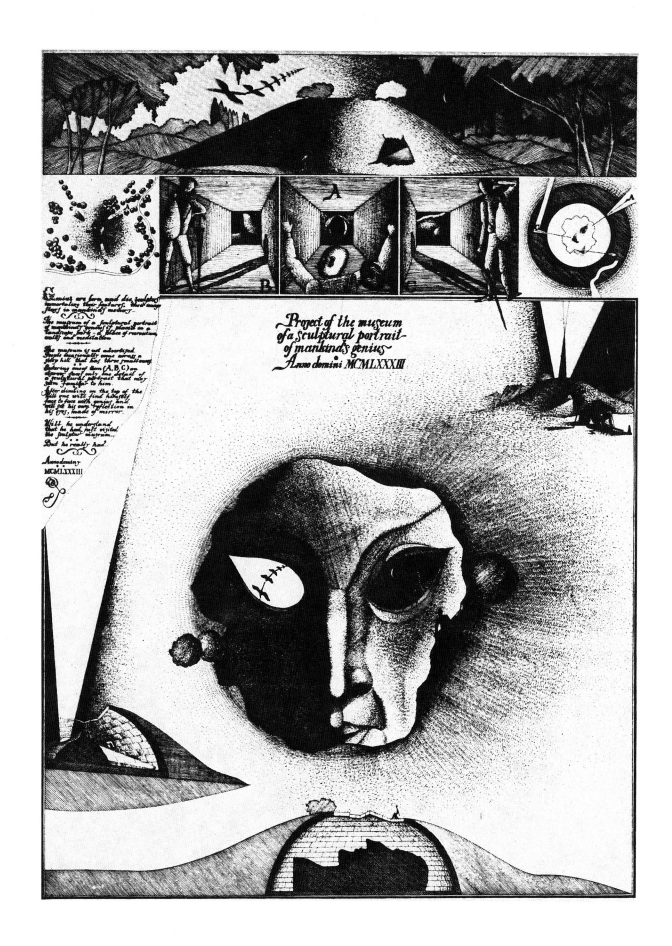

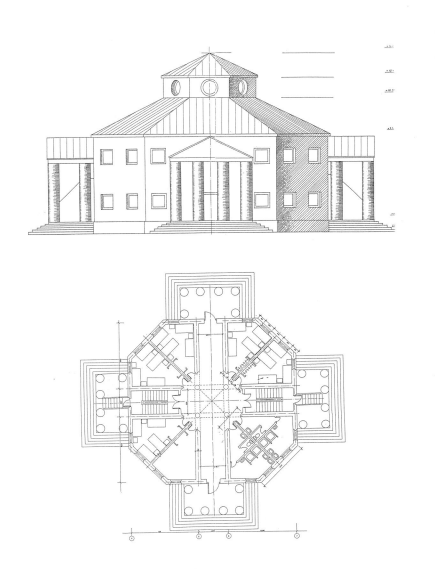

Above and above right: *Lutchik summer camp,* near Moscow, 1989, children's sleeping quarters, facade and plan.

Right: Illustrations of the children's book *Tcheburashka and Crocodile Gena,* 1990.

Opposite: *A Sculpture Museum,* 1983, entry in the Central Glass Company competition in Japan.

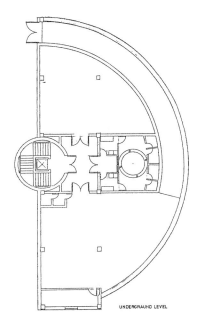

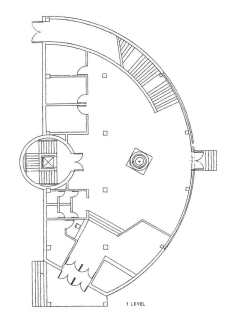

UNDERGRAUND LEVEL

1 LEVEL

Above: *Cultural Initiative Foundation*, Moscow, 1989, perspective and plans.

Below: *Russian Center for Krishna Consciousness Society*, Moscow, 1991, drawings.

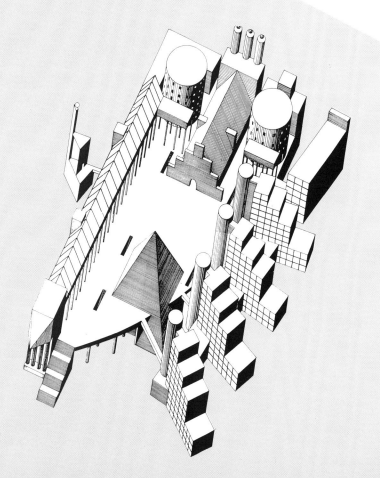

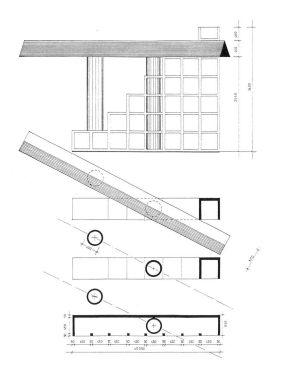

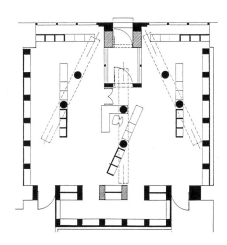

White Hall gallery/store, Moscow,
1990–91, various views.
Above left: Display unit drawing;
above right: floor plan;
below: ceiling plan.

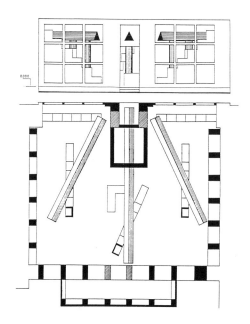

YURI AVVAKUMOV

The Constructivist movement did not survive the 1930s, and different aesthetic ideals have dominated Soviet architectural practice for more than fifty years. With perestroika and democratization, one might expect a renewed interest in the avant-garde tradition. Like the once-repressed names of political leaders that emerge in the press after many years of public oblivion, the works of Constructivism appear ready to start another life, awaiting the reverence of a new generation of art and architectural students. Yet paradoxically, a different aesthetic dominates contemporary Russian art and design. For example, the revolutionary avant-garde has had little influence on the young designers of the Paper Architecture group. The architectural language of their projects seeks inspiration in the urban vernacular, or reflects upon the classical vocabulary of the Russian Empire, and even of Stalinism. With a somewhat perverse confidence, they revere such work for its sense of quality and mastery, both evidently lacking in the uncertain times of the 1990s.

In this context, the works of Yuri Avvakumov and his followers occupy a special place. Born in 1957, Avvakumov went on to graduate from the Moscow Architectural Institute. A member of the Paper Architecture group, and an unofficial theorist and archivist of the movement, he won his first important architectural competition in 1984. The project, called *City as a Club,* was submitted to a competition hosted by the Japanese architecture magazine, *A + U*. From the outset, Avvakumov considered his entry an architectural reinterpretation of the 1920s: "A circus rather than theater, an axonometry rather than a perspective, a barricade rather than a colonnade." In

this proposal, an intricate network of temporary structures was placed in the midst of a typically faceless housing development at the periphery of Moscow. Similar proposals had been made before; it was the style of the inserted elements, with their almost literal paraphrase of Constructivist aesthetics, that created an urban fabric with a new, unexpected character.

The success of this project confirmed Avvakumov's current direction for years; he calls his work "a reflection on the theme of Constructivism." Although he appreciates the skillfulness of Stalinist architecture, he has compared using its heritage to "living in a contaminated hospital ward." Avvakumov's appropriation of the Constructivist idiom is, in typical postmodernist manner, self-consciously superficial and ironic. From a unified amalgam of ideology, theory, and aesthetics, so characteristic of the original Russian avant-garde, he distills only Constructivism's expressive, decorative aspects, devoid of their ideological underpinnings. More importantly, he removes the pathos of the Soviet architectural pioneers, in his belief that Constructivism is "a language not only for composing legends and writing hymns, but also for telling fairy tales and jokes."

Avvakumov's elaborate metal models, which he has been making with different collaborators since 1986, are poignant examples of such architectural "fairy tales." In these compositions he investigates his two particular poetic themes—balance and flying—all the time alluding to particular architectural precedents of the early Russian avant-garde. For example, *Tribune for a Leninist* (1987) takes off from a well-known El Lissitzky sketch of the 1920s. Avvakumov replaces Lissitzky's elevator with a dynamic open staircase, and his version of the structure proclaims "GLASNOST" on a giant screen. Does this postmodernist revision of an early revolutionary project tell us that glasnost itself is but a revision of the 1917 revolution, as critic

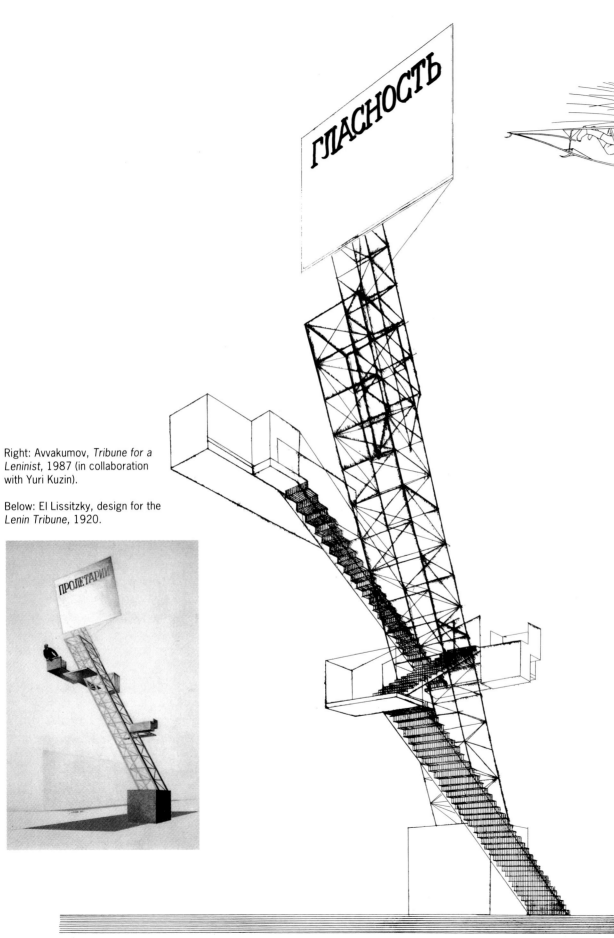

ГЛАСНОСТЬ

Right: Avvakumov, *Tribune for a Leninist,* 1987 (in collaboration with Yuri Kuzin).

Below: El Lissitzky, design for the *Lenin Tribune,* 1920.

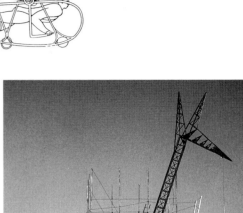

Top: Vladimir Tatlin, *Letatlin,* man-powered glider, 1929–31.

Above: Avvakumov, *Red Tower,* 1987–88 (in collaboration with Yuri Kuzin).

Above: Avvakumov, *Aerobatics*, 1990 (in collaboration with Agitarch Studio).

Michael Govan has suggested? Or is it a formal exploration of the poetic language of Constructivism, a study of mass, transparency, and balance? "I am not interested in political commentaries," says Avvakumov, yet it is not clear if one should take him at his word. An empty leader's tribune, a stair that leads nowhere, a red ship precariously dangling in the air—all these could serve as potent metaphors in the highly charged political atmosphere of Russia today. In this work, the Constructivist balance of masses and planes gives way to the more precarious balance of symbol and form, the verbal and the visual, irony and expression.

Red Tower (1987–88) is designed in homage to *Letatlin,* a bird-like glider built by Vladimir Tatlin in the 1930s. The man-powered flying machine, one of the last works of the aging avant-garde master, was intended for production "as an everyday object for the Soviet masses," yet it never went beyond the prototype stage. Avvakumov's tower consists of construction scaffolding, fire-escape ladders, and a crane, to which the glider is permanently attached, like a dog on a leash. An imposing, somewhat sinister structure seems to provide an excessive, overly elaborate support for the tied-up glider, suggesting the hopelessness of Tatlin's social utopia.

Perestroika Tower (1990) is devoted to a celebrated icon of Socialist Realism: a giant double sculpture of *Worker and Collective Farmer,* created as a centerpiece of Soviet propaganda at the 1937 Paris International Exhibition. Browsing through old architectural magazines, Avvakumov ran across drawings of the sculpture's internal structure. He was fascinated to discover Constructivist skeletons inside the realistic shapes of the figures and set about re-creating the metal structures, surrounding them with dense

wooden scaffolding reminiscent of Tatlin's compositions. The two structural systems seemed to cancel each other out, resulting in a strange pyramidal monumentality, heavy and transparent at the same time. The figures supported by the scaffolding appear to be buried inside, in a precarious standstill that alludes to the designer's interpretation of perestroika.

Scaffolding and fire-escape ladders are favorite construction elements of Avvakumov. "A ladder is one of the first human inventions; it probably precedes the wheel," he claims. "Yet its expressive potential is far from exhausted." Such structures are also low-tech and can be manufactured despite the current economic crisis. In his exhibition designs, Avvakumov uses ladders and found materials to create what he calls "a poverty-based aesthetic." With shortages of the most elementary goods, such ingenuity, sometimes absurdist in character, is required. For an exhibition of work by 1920s Constructivist artist and designer Liubov Popova, Avvakumov and his crew had to make by hand several hundred pieces of special hooks out of nails. Thanks to this effort, the paintings and supporting panels appeared to float gracefully over the simple scaffolding. For an installation accompanying a film festival at the MELZ Club, Avvakumov hung an inverted cupola of steel wire and plastic film inside a pseudo-classical grand hall. A symbol of state power, now empty and deflated, this cupola was complemented with entangled ladders, some of them spread over a pompous red-carpeted stair. The shocking contrast of two visual and semantic systems corresponded well to the sudden shake-up of cultural values, reflected as well by the new Soviet cinematography. Avvakumov's exhibition designs provide an important link between purely conceptual activity and the grim reality of the Soviet architectural profession. His projects offer some consistent aesthetic and methodological clues that can be applied in different formats—from installations to towers, in theory as well as in real construction.

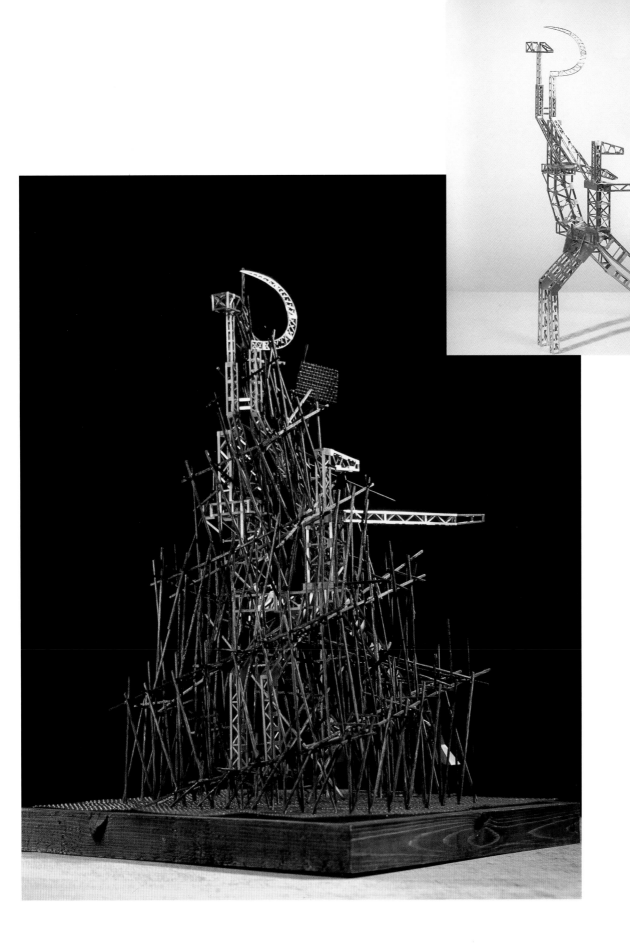

Above: Boris Iofan and Vera Mukhina, *Worker and Collective Farmer*, sculpture for the Soviet Pavillion at the Paris International Exhibition, 1936–37.

Left and top: Avvakumov, *Perestroika Tower*, 1990 (in collaboration with Sergey Podiomschikov and Nikolai Avvakumov).

Above, top and bottom:
Avvakumov, Liubov Popova
exhibition, Moscow, 1989,
various views.

Ever since Yuri Avvakumov ingeniously reappropriated the term "paper architecture" in 1984, he has been collecting projects and documentation on the group's uncoordinated activities. He has always had cool manners and a rare asset of speaking fluent English, and thus has become a major contact between the Moscow architectural scene and a host of Western curators, collectors, and journalists interested in Russian culture.

Avvakumov's projects will inevitably be compared to the work of his Western counterparts: architects grouped under the banner of Deconstructivism. While each of them follows their own highly subjective creative trajectory, Avvakumov's work is deeply rooted in his Russian heritage. If one is to believe historian Catherine Cooke, the adepts of Deconstructivism "can be seen as using the oeuvre of Leonidov exactly as he and fellow Constructivists would have desired." Perhaps the avant-garde masters would have been happier still with the projects of Avvakumov. Although he does not spearhead an alternative movement, his works offer a possible option for new forms of architectural expressions. His is a necessary and very timely task in a newly liberated Russian culture.

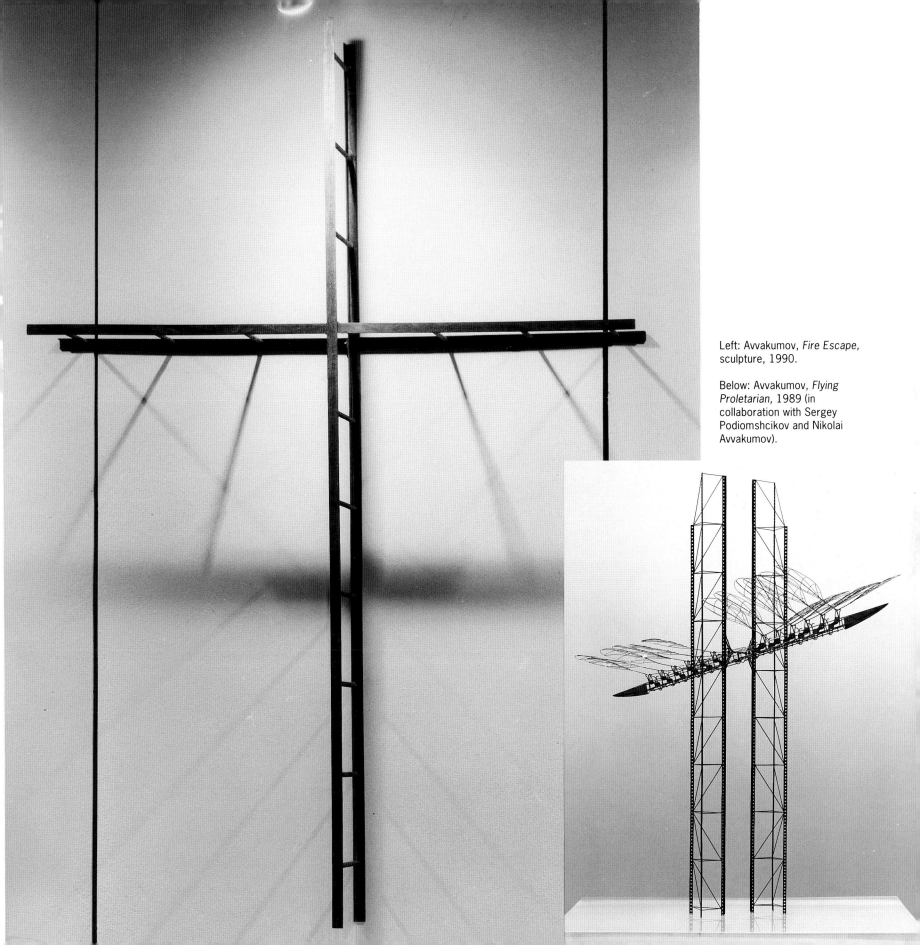

Left: Avvakumov, *Fire Escape*, sculpture, 1990.

Below: Avvakumov, *Flying Proletarian*, 1989 (in collaboration with Sergey Podiomshcikov and Nikolai Avvakumov).

Above and right: Avvakumov, Installation at the MELZ Club, Moscow, 1989 (in collaboration with Agitarch Studio).

Above, left and right: Avvakumov,
Installation at the ASSA exhibition,
Moscow, 1988 (in collaboration
with Sergey Shutov).

Near right: Avvakumov, Poster for
the German Theater Festival,
Moscow, 1989.

Far right: Avvakumov, Poster for
the IUA Congress, 1987.

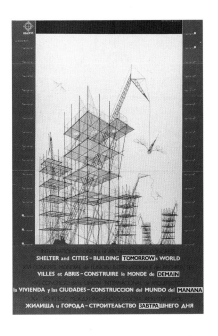

ART-BLYA

For more than fifty years, the myth of the sacred state border served as a cornerstone of Soviet propaganda. For the West, the Iron Curtain was a tangible manifestation of the Cold War, and the Berlin Wall became its most dramatic symbol. A hardened Soviet society created its own invisible barriers: these took the form of censorship, obligatory residence registration, passport control, and records of work activity.

The young architectural group Art-Blya, on the other hand, seems to defy the very notion of barriers. Its work does not contain anything openly subversive, yet its existence would hardly be possible in the pre-glasnost era. Art-Blya is a loose collective of friends that includes architects, artists, musicians, poets, and filmmakers. Its three founding members orchestrate most of their activities from a tiny basement studio located in an enormous Stalinist-era building in the center of Moscow. Co-founders Mikhail Labazov and Andrey Savin, both born in 1961, and Andrey Cheltsov, one year older, all graduated from Moscow Architectural Institute together in 1985. About fifteen people have participated in the group's projects since it was established in 1986.

This is how the group explains its name: "Art means art . . . The less people try to describe the meaning of art, the better. And Blya? It's slang, meaning frustration and happiness at the same time. Despair and delight. It helps when one runs out of words." According to its multidisciplinary constituents, Art-Blya attempts to abolish borders between artistic disciplines. In 1990 the group created an unusual exhibition devoted to young Moscow architects. The projects were reproduced on sheets of glass, which were then assembled into a monumental fourteen-foot tower. A month later, at the closing of the show,

the tower was shattered into pieces and buried: the entire event was videotaped and turned into a film. Was this glass tower a piece of exhibit design, a work of art, or an act of theater? Art-Blya believes that architecture should include all these definitions, combining objects, space, and action into one fluid, continuous experience.

The group's architectural and design projects are often characterized by flexible lines and generated by an interpenetration of different environments and substances. *Country House* (1987) has a conventional core, enveloped with inflatable membrane walls. Unlike the taut futuristic inflatables of the Radical Architecture movement, these walls have an uncertain shape and subtle fluctuations: they relate the house to the natural phenomena of clouds, trees, and haystacks. In another project, a wide wooden board gradually turns into a chair. The chair is conceived of as a process, as a series of consecutive states, rather than as a single finalized product.

Art-Blya members have created a number of complex urbanist proposals. For them, the city is an artificial landscape that, like an abandoned building, can be put to many uses. They pay particular attention to the space between structures. "Space is not a passive vacuum," reads an Art-Blya project proposal. "One should feel space, experience it, use it as a vital life function, the way air is used for breathing." The project proposed an ephemeral structure of wires and stretched trusses that would fill the negative space of the city. People would be held with ropes, and would move with the help of simple mechanical devices, "very much like birds." The air would contain a theater, a zoo, even a swimming pool. Like a colorful three-dimensional carnival, this flexible net would hover just above the hard urban structure. Most Russian architects, who still retain a notion of the city as a fixed combination of buildings, streets, and squares, would dismiss this idea as nonsense. It is not

Above: Savin and Labazov, *Country House*, 1987, project.

Savin, *The Space of Communications*, 1989, project. Near right and far right: Conceptual rendering for proposed site; below: plan.

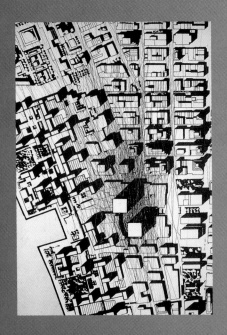

far, though, from the postmodernist interpretation of the phenomenon of the metropolis. In the book *The Hot House*, Andrea Branzi regards the urban environment as "a sort of liquid space in which we are all immersed like fish in the sea, which forms part of our own bodily rather than mental experience." Although Moscow possesses many of the qualities of a metropolis, Art-Blya chose New York as the site for its proposal. Ever since Malevich pasted up a rendering of his *Architekton* on the Manhattan skyline, the New York landscape has, in the eyes of Russian architects, represented an idealized background for testing bold ideas.

Even though the activities of Art-Blya appear to be purely conceptual, in 1988 the group won a coveted architectural competition for a real building—a memorial museum to Vladimir Vysotsky. The untimely death of this popular anti-establishment bard has lifted him to the rank of cultural super-hero. The winning project, however, returns to the original earthly simplicity associated with Vysotsky's songs. Art-Blya attempted to go beyond the familiar stereotype of the museum as an isolated building. Remembering the basic definition of architecture as an organization of space, the group members referred

to an existing space between two old houses on the site. The museum grows out of a typical Moscow courtyard—an important setting for many of Vysotsky's narratives—framed with a long gallery wall, and it accommodates a permanent exhibition space and a flexible stage. A tree, garden benches, a red brick wall—urban objects full of special significance in everyday Russian life—become integral parts of the museum, in much the same way that common artifacts formed part of the environment in the visionary *Space Settlements* project.

The Vysotsky building's fate has sadly been marred by a long bureaucratic battle over the museum's construction. Several mandatory revisions have already violated the clarity of the original solution, yet no progress is in sight. In fact, the architects have lost hope in the project ever being completed. It seems this last border—from theoretical visionary work to the reality of Russian professional practice—is one the group has not yet been willing to cross. The written statement of Art-Blya once included the optimistic note, "Today we've got a number of ideas, and an unexpected chance to implement them." This line of text has now been carefully crossed out.

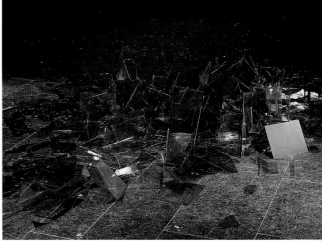

Above and left: Savin, Labazov, and Pavlova, *Glass Tower*, erected and destroyed, executed for the Young Moscow Architects exhibition, 1990.

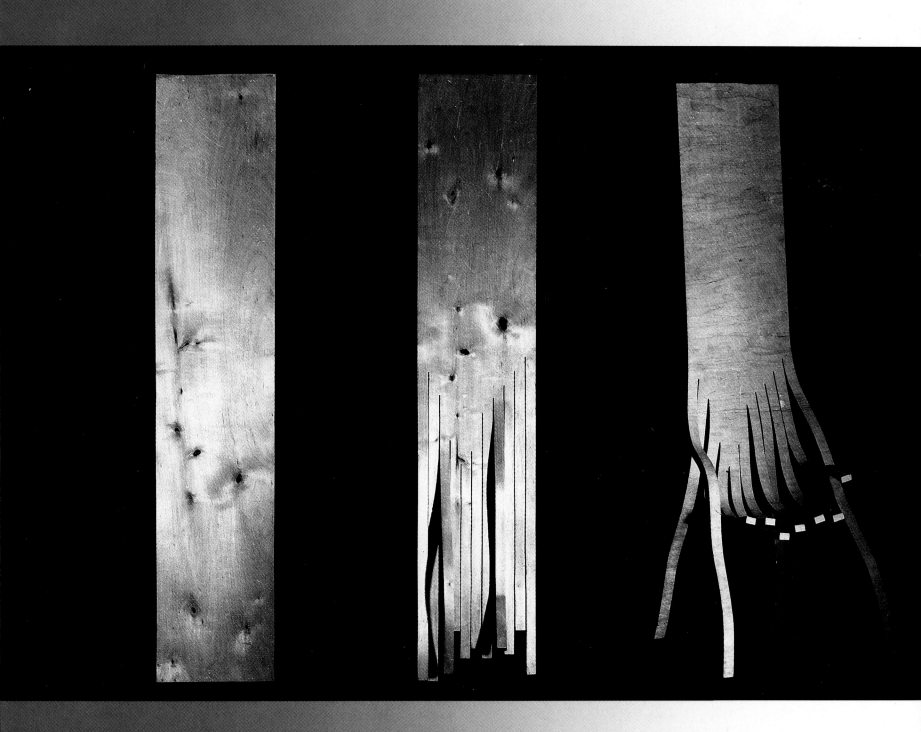

Opposite: Savin, *Wood Board Chair*, 1987, three stages of construction.

Right: Savin, *Double Member Scissors*, 1989, competition project.

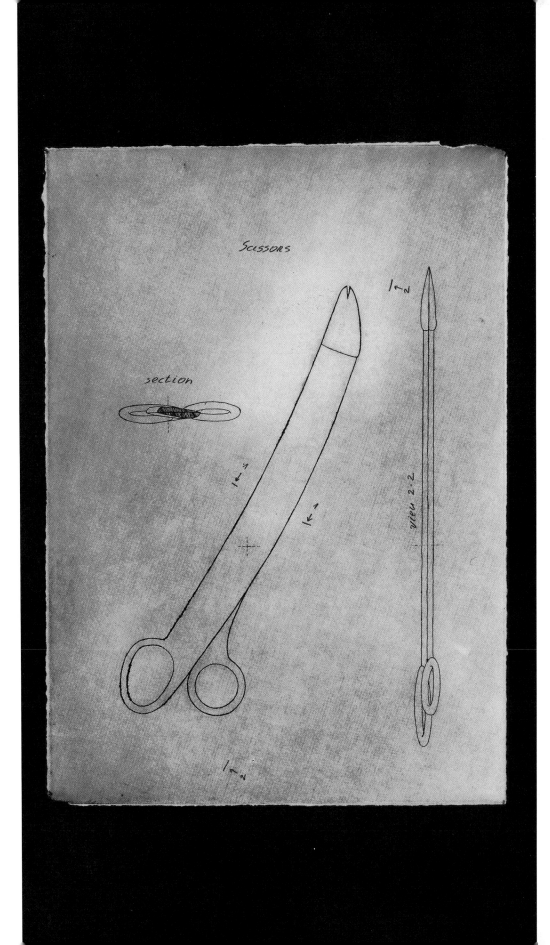

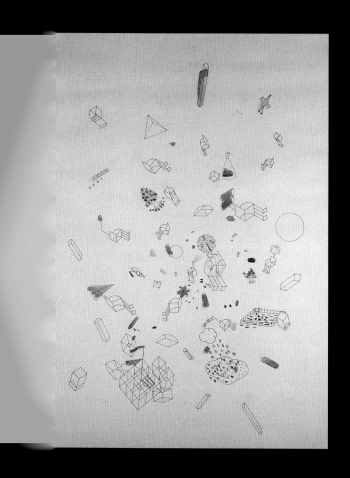

Above: Savin and Labazov, *Space Settlements*, collage, 1989.

Above left: Labazov and collaborators, *Space of the Twenty-first Century*, 1988, project.

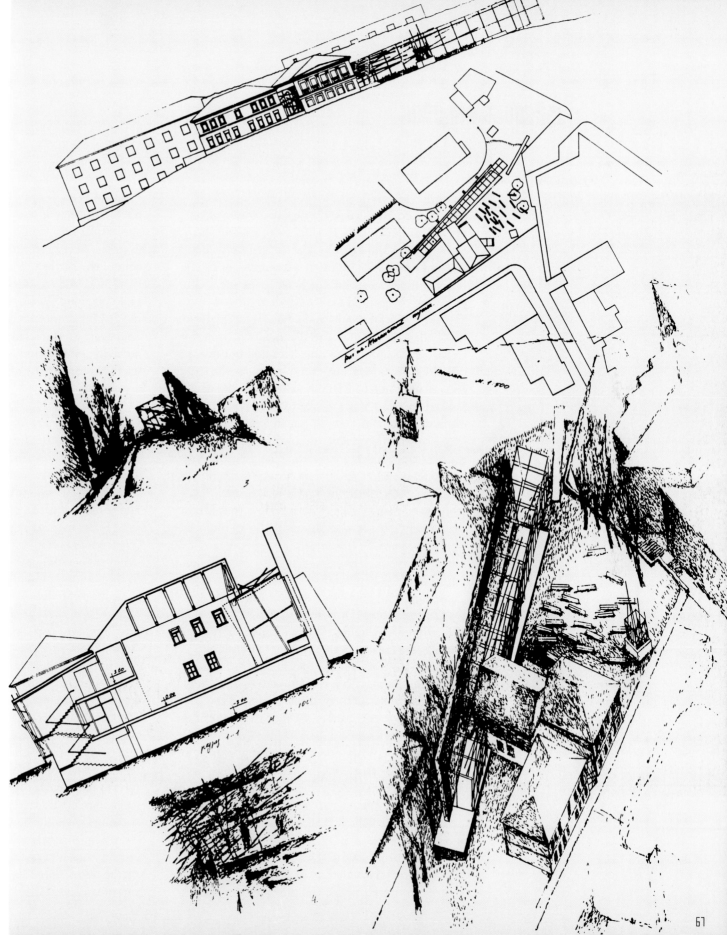

Above: Savin and Labazov,
Wooden Tower, installation, Kotka,
Finland, 1990.

Right: Labazov and Savin,
*Memorial Museum to Vladimir
Vysotsky,* Moscow, 1988,
drawings.

ISKANDER GALIMOV

Since the beginning of the twentieth century, the term "eclecticism" has had a negative connotation in the Russian cultural lexicon. Beginning in the 1830s, the aesthetic system of eclecticism provided a range of options for an increased number of clients, undermining the monolith of classicism and preparing the ground for the Modern movement. The early Russian avant-garde, however, eagerly got rid of what they regarded as this holdover from the Czarist era. Socialist Realism also could not tolerate the variety of expressions found in pre-revolutionary architectural practice. In the 1980s, as echoes of Western postmodernist discourse reached Soviet professional circles, there appeared a renewed interest in the concept of eclecticism. In the context of glasnost this concept even assumed a political connotation. After years of proscribed aesthetic directions, the very ability to browse through the world's styles and cultural treasures and to combine them freely in one's work amounted to an important step toward artistic freedom.

For Iskander Galimov, such encylopedic eclecticism informs not only the content of his works, but his entire professional position. To some, he is a serious academic researcher; to others, a facile architectural illustrator, a creator of trendy, if not gimmicky, images. Galimov would not reject either of these labels. Graduating from the Moscow Architectural Institute in 1983, he successfully participated in a number of competitions and joined the ranks of the Paper Architecture movement. At the same time he was completing work on his doctorate, in which he put forward esoteric concepts regarding "the perceptual language of architecture." In his thesis he attempts to synthesize two major notions of perception: the Gestalt theory, which puts the integral structure of an image prior to its constituent parts, and the structuralist cognitive theory, which allows for subdivision of an image into a number of simple, atomic elements. Galimov's drawings are

supplied as an illustrative accompaniment to his doctorate, but the relationship between his bizarre, spectacular images and the text is not obvious. For example, *Templecity* shows an enormous, city-like ruin of the Parthenon composed of full-size buildings of all styles, taken directly from the pages of a history of architecture. *Viaducity* has similar "building blocks" piled into the shape of a giant Roman aqueduct. An exuberant design for a contemporary architectural museum is somewhat more tangible, as it is based on the use of scale models arranged around a vast pool.

Galimov's visionary drawings go beyond the structural and semantic complexity normally associated with postmodernist architectural thinking. They are closer in spirit to sixteenth-century Italian mannerism, with its artistic intricacy, abundance and density of detail, and show of stylistic mastery. John Shearman's definition of mannerism— "complexity and invention that are the result of deliberately raising difficulties, so that dexterity may be displayed in overcoming them"—is well suited to Galimov's style.

The architect's particular affinity lies with Arcimboldo, an Italian mannerist painter who from 1562 to 1587 worked at the court of the Austrian Hapsburgs in Vienna and Prague. Arcimboldo gained reverence and fame for painting "composed heads," allegorical portraits that were assembled with fruits, vegetables, flowers, stones, even roasted game. The analysis of Arcimboldo's work by Roland Barthes could as well apply to Galimov. The structure of human language is twice articulated, says Barthes; it can be broken down first into words, which have meaning, then into sounds, which signify nothing. Generally, this structure does not apply to visual arts and architecture: one can only break down the pictorial image into lines and points that have no meaning of their own. Arcimboldo's (and Galimov's)

~ TEMPLE·CITY ~

But clocks tick on, and seasons come and go,
The names of cities change, rents retain
No witnesses, and memories and tears
May not be shared... Unmarked and unsought,
The shades of loved ones shrink and slip away,
And we recoil in horror from the thought
That they might reappear...

...We realise that we no longer know where lies the path
To that lone house, and even as in a dream,
Despairing, made, to where it stood, and lo! —
Discover that the walls, the things, the columns
Are different and strange, and that we too
Are strangers there...

Anna Akhmatova

69

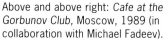
Above and above right: *Cafe at the Gorbunov Club,* Moscow, 1989 (in collaboration with Michael Fadeev).

Opposite: *Contemporary Architectural-Art Museum,* 1988.

work makes drawing into a genuine language, giving it a double articulation by subdividing it into the forms of nameable and recognizable objects. In addition to the denoted, obvious meaning of every element in one of Galimov's drawings, there is also a whole range of connotations. Consequently, his complex, multifaceted drawings have become symbols of the Paper Architecture movement, often placed on catalogue covers and exhibition posters of the group.

The beauty of nature lies in its unity, writes Barthes, therefore the decomposition of forms into elements normally creates a disturbing, unhealthy impression—"a malaise of matter." The visionary projects of Galimov do give the eerie sensation of an architectural swarm. He would have to overcome this in his commissioned work. A project for the Russian Center in Bologna, Italy (1989), designed in collaboration

with Michael Fadeev, successfully organizes diverse architectural elements into the shape of a fairy-tale ship. The resulting intricate silhouette has many precedents in Russian architecture, recalling the composition of cathedrals and monasteries. Unique among his peers, Galimov has managed to combine the decorative language of medieval Russia with a contemporary architectural bent.

The question of the feasibility of his architecture, however, remains open. The interior of a cafe at Gorbunov Club in Moscow (1989) looks rigidly classicist compared to the wondrous diversity of his architectural fantasies. Galimov's favorite architects, he confesses, "all belong to the 'right-wing' avant-garde: Rossi, Graves, Leon Krier." The classicizing tendency, always present in Galimov's work, will not, one hopes, come to dominate his mysterious and original work.

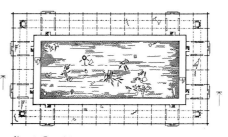

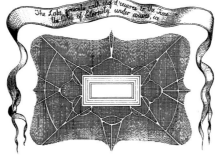

Outer view.

The Lake, ground with shed'd œuvres in the Time the hint of Eternity under waves, ice.

Ground Floor Plan . 1:1000

71

VIADUCITY

Above: *Viaducity*, 1987 (in
collaboration with Michail Fadeev).

Opposite: *Cathedral*.

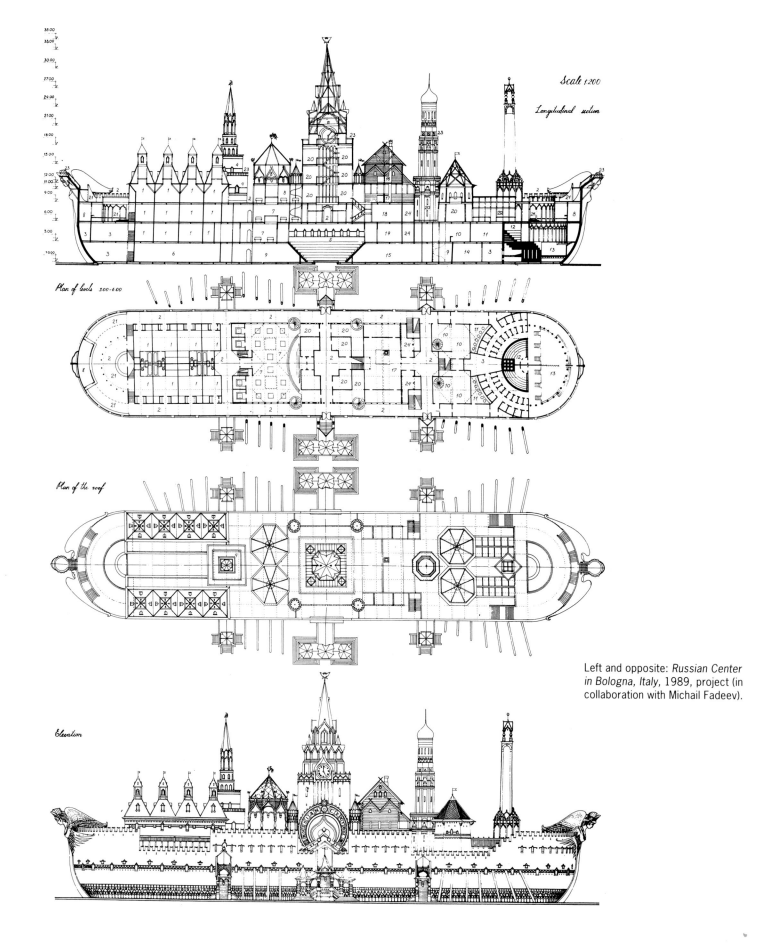

Scale 1:200

Longitudinal section

Plan of levels 3.00-6.00

Plan of the roof

Elevation

Left and opposite: *Russian Center in Bologna, Italy*, 1989, project (in collaboration with Michail Fadeev).

74

ALEXANDER ERMOLAEV AND STUDIO TAF

In September 1989, a large United States Information Agency exhibition of American design started its tour of nine major Russian cities. Visitors' reactions were duly documented in a guest book. Most responses looked enviously at American design. "Thanks for giving us a glimpse of the twenty-first century, we're still living in the nineteenth," read one comment. "You have a life and we live in hell," noted another. "Thank you for reminding me that I live in a cave," wrote a third observer. Obviously many visitors, frustrated and tired of their living and working conditions, were ready to discard their lifestyles altogether in a unanimous embrace of Western cultural values.

Alexander Ermolaev does not share this sentiment. He engages in what he calls "design for survival," a concept that is motivated by and draws inspiration from the misery of the Russian cultural environment. "Life in here is peculiar," he explains. "The absence of contemporary materials and technologies forces designers to develop an ability to work with that little that they have, and to turn it into truly artistic work. The designer learns how to 'survive' and teaches this skill to others. Most importantly, he learns how to get pleasure out of the whole process."

One comment Ermolaev might agree with is the remark about living in a cave. He once gave an assignment to his students to rebuild a cave—a Northern coal mine. The students interpreted the project as a provocation, a call for action. To express their ideas architecturally, they proposed a number of absurd interventions: unusable furniture, electronic and mechanical scarecrows, circulation obstacles,

twisted communication lines. Why? "To provoke the workers to recognize the necessity of creative change. To make them suddenly feel free, living without orders and directives . . . to liberate their conscience," explained the participants. The spirit of the early Russian avant-garde resounds in this statement: it is a similar critical attitude Ermolaev encourages.

An architect by education, Ermolaev started to work in design in the early 1960s. He joined the team of VNIITE, then a newly established institution of Soviet design. From the beginning, he manifested an interest in alternative design sources and materials. He envisioned an experimental toy block system in which rigid and soft parts could be put together to form various micro-environments for children. His radical concept of ad-hoc wooden furniture called for self-assembly with an assortment of scrap wood: shortages and high costs, routinely associated with traditional furniture production, were thus circumvented. These projects, like so many others at VNIITE, ended up as prototypes, never to be put into production. In 1975, Ermolaev was instrumental in developing an installation for the Ninth ICSID Congress in Moscow, at which he planned to present radical cardboard furniture and fragmented graphics. When most of the program was cancelled on the grounds that it was not representative, he left VNIITE, forever abandoning his official design career.

Shortly thereafter, Ermolaev started a children's studio named TAF (Theater of Architectural Form). For years, while supporting himself through teaching a conventional course at the Moscow Architectural Institute, he had been giving his heart and all his spare time to the studio. Now, Ermolaev has built TAF into an independent group of young architects, designers, and artists who conduct research and organize exhibitions. The studio claims to have a "collective mind," to act as a creative commune, yet it

Top left: Evgeny Koval/Studio TAF, Coat rack, 1990–91.

Top right: Evgeny Koval/Studio TAF, Outdoor light, 1990–91.

Bottom left: Evgeny Koval/Studio TAF, Chair, 1990–91.

Bottom right: Yuri Kuznetsov and Kirill Gladky/Studio TAF, Workstation, 1990–91.

Alexander Ermolaev/Studio TAF, Permanent installation at the history museum of the town of Pechory, 1990. Above: *Room of Anxiety*, representing the Soviet period from 1950 to the 1970s; above right: *Room of Hope*, representing the future of the town; near right and far right: details of the installation; opposite: *Room of Genius Loci*, representing the ancient history of the region.

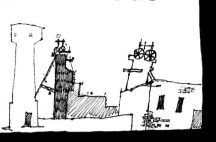

Left: Alexander Ermolaev/Studio TAF, Design for an Inta coal mine, 1990–91.

remains a populist dictatorship rather than a true democracy. Ermolaev's maverick personality clearly dominates the group's artistic activity.

During the 1980s, TAF investigated a fundamental concept of Ermolaev's, what he has called "the poetry of the casual." In this view, everything can become a design material: objects of everyday life, industrial scrap, family memories, the heritage of a favorite architect. Thus for a year group members studied the work of avant-garde master Vladimir Tatlin: they re-created his counter-reliefs with contemporary materials, wrote a script based on imaginary letters by him, and made a collective attempt to build a version of his legendary tower. The new post-perestroika concept of "design for survival" involves more somber and socially concerned work, a response to the country's deep economic crisis.

Junk, salvaged materials, and urban refuse were used extensively during the 1980s by a number of alternative Western European designers, notably in Great Britain and Germany. Their experiments constituted an effective critique of the rational approach in architecture and product design. The projects of Ermolaev's group are critical of their own roots, calling attention to the lower depths of everyday Russian life. Yet at the same time they exonerate this very reality, in that throw-away matter, forms, and images are acknowledged as a relevant source of inspiration. In this sense, scholar Oleg Genisaretsky defines the group's work as part of an "ecological avant-garde." Ex-TAF member Elza Okina thus interprets a lamp from the group's last exhibition: "In a certain respect, this object could be a symbol of all Russian design, so clunky and ridiculous does it look. Viewed another way, it is full of compassion toward its own absurdity. This project does not represent an outsider's position: it

is a view from somebody who is right inside our system, and who cares about it."

Still, Ermolaev faces a lot of criticism within the Russian design community. Many find his aesthetic of poverty, or "Ermolaevness," as it has become known, to be alienating and antipopulist. There is also a concern about the practical viability of his concepts. Ermolaev has long called himself a "designer-diagnostician," one whose job is to point out problems, but to leave the solving of those problems to others. In fact, he has usually shown a rather loose methodology; his project solutions are rarely complete. Lately, though, he has been willing to prove that he is ready to engage in actual professional practice. He and Studio TAF have collaborated on a permanent installation for the history museum in the northern Russian town of Pechory, known for its ancient cave monastery. Each room of the museum is designed in a different style in order to better transmit the spirit of different historical epochs. The so-called Room of Anxiety, for instance, is devoted to the Soviet period of the 1950s–1970s. Along with samples of propaganda, police barriers, and other threatening artifacts of the time, one can see undistinguished clothes from a local weaving mill, pressed between sheets of glass. The museum installation was a fortunate assignment for Ermolaev and his studio as it allowed them to implement their long-held theories, and to to make a highly personalized selection of objects into expressive narrative compositions.

Perhaps Ermolaev and Studio TAF will always remain on the fringe of Russian design. A special, educated breed of clients—which hardly exists in Russia today—is required to move their "design for survival" from studios and classrooms into the reality of everyday life.

Above: Kirill Gladky/Studio TAF, Lamp, 1990–91.

Above right: Studio TAF exhibition, Moscow, 1991.

Near right: Tania Shulika/Studio TAF, Object, 1990–91.

Far right: Kostia Shulika/Studio TAF, Dish-rack, 1990–91.

Below: Studio TAF exhibition, Moscow, 1991.

Below right: Evgeny Koval/Studio TAF, Illuminated sign, 1990–91.

Above and right: Studio TAF, Desk organizers, 1990–91.

Opposite, top: Alexander Ermolaev/Studio TAF, Set for the "Capital Show" television program—the Russian equivalent of "Wheel of Fortune."

Opposite, bottom: Alexander Ermolaev/Studio TAF, Design for an Inta coal mine, 1990–91, detail of drawing.

EVGENY AMASPUR

In the center of Moscow, in the courtyard of the former KGB headquarters, sits a most unexpected and unconventional building—the Mayakovsky Museum, an imaginative creation by designer Evgeny Amaspur. Mayakovsky was a major Russian poet of the first half of this century. Once officially hailed as the perfect embodiment of the socialist poet, he remains genuinely popular in many parts of Russian society. Like most members of the Russian avant-garde, he welcomed the revolution, and wrote of the new system in a brilliant, highly personal poetic style. A maverick personality, he exerted considerable influence on the art, literature, and social life of his time. A small, unprepossessing room was Mayakovsky's official residence. It was there that he took his own life in 1930, tired of growing artistic and political pressure and a series of unhappy love affairs. The first Mayakovsky Museum, however, was established at a different place, in the apartment of literary critics Lila and Osip Brik; the poet actually had lived there for years, a lover of Lila and a friend/confidant of Osip. By the 1950s, a campaign was mounted against the role of the Briks in Mayakovsky's life. Their Jewishness and the strange love triangle involving Mayakovsky did not fit the stereotypical cultural myth of a great Russian poet, and history was promptly rewritten in typical Soviet fashion.

The museum was eventually moved into Mayakovsky's official residence. It was a lifeless, vacuous place; almost nothing of the poet's had been preserved on the site. The director arranged for temporary exhibitions in order to enliven the space and to attract the attention of the public. Toward this end, she brought in Evgeny Amaspur. Born in 1945, Amaspur graduated from the Moscow Stroganoff Art School. There, he discovered the then-fashionable hyper-realist style of painting, which became his passion for many years ahead. Evgeny aspired to work in theater as a stage designer. Instead he found a position at KDOI, a state agency of decorative arts, where he was responsible for installing several artistic and propaganda exhibitions. In the early 1980s, Amaspur designed "Mayakovsky and Folk Art," the popularity of which prompted a series of shows devoted to some previously unexplored aspects of the poet's life and work. The utilization of early Russian avant-garde language, a fresh perspective on familiar figures in Soviet literature, and the overall sophistication of these exhibitions made the museum a special place during the uneventful late years of Brezhnev's rule.

In the meantime, the new wings of the expanded KGB headquarters were being constructed around the museum building. A dangerous crack developed in the nearly vacated house. The house would have been doomed had this happened a decade earlier; in the mid-eighties, though, different sentiments were in the air. In an unprecedented decision, the KGB agreed to offer the entire four-story building to the museum, and to arrange for a complete renovation, even providing its own construction team. A group of designers, including Amaspur, was assigned to work on this vast project. With Machiavellian tactics, he managed to get rid of his collaborators/competitors, and committed himself over the next four years to envisioning and implementing a design on his own.

"I invented this museum. It had been dead, and I gave it life," says Amaspur, sitting in an antique throne-like chair in his vaulted spacious studio. In particular, he regards the interior as his personal artistic expression, a "painting in space." Two strategies are crucial in his design method: narrative and metaphor. Mayakovsky's own life provides an exciting narrative, and its development is arranged spatially. The first floor, with its low ceilings and grotesque dark atmosphere, takes the visitor through the

Permanent installation at the
Mayakovsky Museum, Moscow,
1986–89 (in collaboration with
Andrey Bokov, architect, and Taras
Polyakov, writer). Left: *Central
staircase;* opposite: *Mayakovsky's
Pre-revolutionary Cubo-Futurist
Activity.* Photographs by Yuri
Palmin.

Opposite: Permanent installation at
the Mayakovsky Museum, Moscow,
1986–89 (in collaboration with
Andrey Bokov, architect, and Taras
Polyakov, writer), various views.

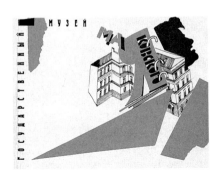

Above: Promotional material for the
Mayakovsky Museum, Moscow,
with YA (I) graphic symbol of the
artistic ego.

prerevolutionary years of Mayakovsky's life. Upon
reaching the year 1919 on the narrative time scale
(when the poet first moved into the building), the
visitor is positioned at the bottom of the original
staircase, which he must climb to view the spiritual
center of the museum—the carefully restored room
on the fourth floor where Mayakovsky lived and
worked. This area gives way to an abstract open
space, where long curving ramps transport the visitor
into a world where the attempt to *build* poetry is made.

The installation is rich in visual referents. The
metaphor, an important element of Mayakovsky's
poetry, is often *physically* rendered. The staircase, for
instance, is a metaphor of artistic ascent and
aspiration, with fragments from the past and the
future interspersed along the landings and
semitransparent walls. An oversized chair-throne, not
unlike Amaspur's own, serves as a symbol of power
and institution. Here it is filled with memorial busts
and souvenir statuettes of the poet, questioning this
dubious and superficial form of homage. Near the
constructed deathbed of the poet, multiplied faces of
his not-so-faithful followers cover the partitions like
wallpaper to further emphasize Mayakovsky's unique
influence. Even absence becomes metaphor, as in the

zone devoted to the stagnation of the 1970s, with
empty dark-brown walls, devoid of any displays.

Amaspur's design incorporates numerous historical
documents, artifacts, and personal objects of
Mayakovsky and his contemporaries. These items are
inserted, often rather violently, into the personalized
artistic framework of Amaspur's sets. The glass that
encases these objects is typically shattered, charred, or
worked over. Where Amaspur exhibits a certain
document as bent or torn, it is commonly replaced
with a facsimile. Such easy interchangeability of the
real, the fabricated, and the imagined, the exuberance
of this simulated world of constructed metaphors,
takes the museum to the level of a cultural
Disneyland.

Such an irreverent attitude to cultural treasures has
brought its share of criticism. Amaspur has a lot of
enemies. His refusal to compromise, his shrewd and
defiant character, and his persistent tactics have all
contributed to his controversial reputation. A case in
point: The street facade of the Mayakovsky museum
emphasizes a huge single letter in the poet's name.
This letter—which means "I," or "ego," in Russian—
is a very important one for Amaspur as well.

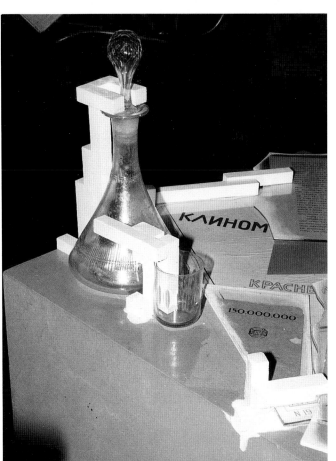

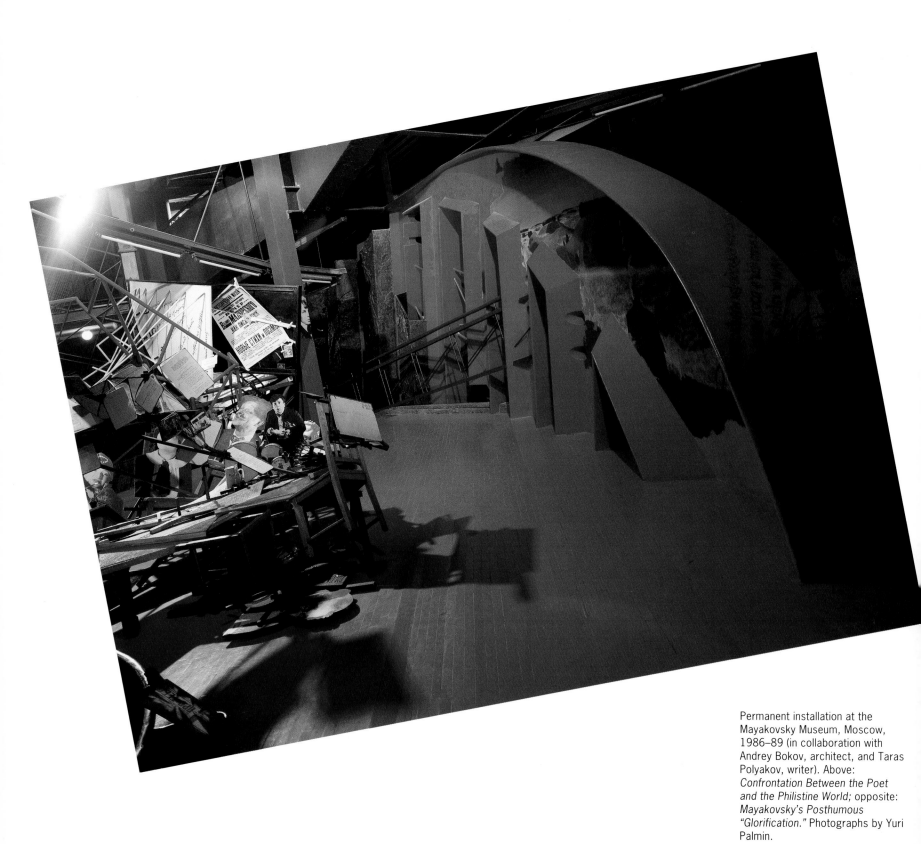

Permanent installation at the Mayakovsky Museum, Moscow, 1986–89 (in collaboration with Andrey Bokov, architect, and Taras Polyakov, writer). Above: *Confrontation Between the Poet and the Philistine World;* opposite: *Mayakovsky's Posthumous "Glorification."* Photographs by Yuri Palmin.

EVGENY BOGDANOV and STAS TCHERMENSKY

In 1787, the Russian empress Catherine the Great made a trip to the southern regions of the country. Traveling with a brilliant entourage, she sought to ascertain the prosperity of the new territories, which were added to the empire after a successful war with the Turks. Legend has it that Prince Potemkin, a governor of the region, built fake villages along the empress's route, with attractive two-dimensional fronts facing the road. The villages were designed to impress the empress and her guests with Potemkin's accomplishments in colonizing the area. His success was twofold. Catherine showered him with awards and titles, and he entered history as the originator of the Potemkin Village, a symbol of any sham project, created for show and self-promotion.

According to design critic Oleg Genisaretsky, Potemkin Villages established an important precedent for all Russian culture. Indeed, exhibitions like it were a fundamental aspect of the Soviet system, reflected in its economy, foreign affairs, and scientific and cultural endeavors. The grounds of the Exhibition of National Economic Achievements (VDNKh) could serve as a glittering example. In this vast Disneyland of socialist propaganda, the concept of a victorious and prosperous socialist state was actually materialized. Another essential display item—Lenin's body—was embalmed and publicly exhibited in a mausoleum to assure the continuity of his revolutionary teaching. Army parades twice a year demonstrated hundreds of tanks, missiles, and other weaponry to illustrate a military power of the country. Portraits of party leaders decorated major buildings for the holidays. An observer might conclude that displaying the icons of the Soviet system was essential for its very existence.

No wonder the mammoth task of creating displays and exhibitions around the country has traditionally occupied many designers, artists, and architects. Such was the case for Evgeny Bogdanov and Stas Tchermensky, who in 1980 joined forces at KDOI, the state agency of decorative arts that distributed commissions on exhibits and public interior design. Bogdanov was born in 1946; after graduating from the Stroganoff Art School in Moscow he spent several years working at the main design institution of the Soviet Union, VNIITE. He was one of the principal designers of the explosive installation for the 1975 Congress of ICSID in Moscow, which was eventually censored by the authorities. Soon after, Bogdanov left VNIITE and began to work in exhibition design. Tchermensky, born in 1950, also studied at the Stroganoff Art School. Exhibition design attracted them with its relative creative freedom, unusual in the Brezhnev era. Although the themes and content of all shows had to be approved and checked, the formulas that censors applied to test a work of art for its socialist spirit did not clearly extend into the field of exhibition design. Often, the ephemeral nature and limited audiences of exhibitions lessened the attention paid to them by the authorities. With cunning and sophistication, designers came to use the situation to their benefit, turning would-be propaganda shows into memorable artistic environments.

The exhibition designs of Bogdanov and Tchermensky are not mere support systems. "Art for art's sake" is the closest approximation of their attitude. Their spatial constructions are indeed meant to demonstrate themselves more than the intended materials of a given show. From the beginning, they developed an analytical method, based on the collage of three independent elements: objects for display,

Right: Velimir Khlebnikov Centennial
Exhibition, Moscow, 1985,
installation on Mayakovsky.

method of display, and interior space. According to the designers, the three do not have to relate in a continuous, harmonious way. The objects of exhibition might be as tepid as propaganda brochures or military regalia; the space, tight and unsuitable. Juxtaposing heterogeneous components, Bogdanov and Tchermensky would come up with an installation that turned the whole into a dramatic, if not absurdist set. Only this method could save them when the subject matter was something like "Activity Of Communist Party Cells at Shoe Factory." Another such example was an exhibition of Leninist literature in Moscow. Virtually the entire hall was occupied by a bright red Constructivist structure, which prevented movement across the space. Lenin's books and booklets, placed by the walls, were effectively reduced to superficial ornaments.

In 1984 Bogdanov and Tchermensky worked on an exhibition of Production Art. Early in the 1920s, the theorists of Production Art claimed that the purpose of all artistic activity was the production of useful objects. Eventually, many of the postulates of this group were adopted by the Constructivists and used in the design of experimental architecture, products, and clothing. Following in their predecessors' footsteps, Bogdanov and Tchermensky themselves fashioned numerous display objects. Monumental fragments of early avant-garde architecture and Constructivist-inspired tables and shelves were as much a part of the show as the historical material on display. Because of the designers' reverent attitude toward Constructivism, they sought a closer integration of subject matter with exposition system. "Constructivism is an aspiration toward clear and intelligible coordinates," says Bogdanov. "it is exciting to see it being projected onto today's reality." The show had a special section on contemporary followers of Constructivism, which included the work of Bogdanov and Tchermensky themselves. A curious historical continuity was evident throughout, since

many canonical works of Constructivist design, such as Rodchenko's Workers' Club, were also built only for display at international fairs. In effect, the two designers have been creating "exhibitions of exhibitions"; this is perhaps the most accurate way to preserve the memory of the Russian avant-garde.

One of the most complex projects by the designers—a centennial exhibition honoring Velimir Khlebnikov—was installed at a literary museum in Moscow in 1985. A visionary poet and philosopher working at the beginning of the twentieth century, Khlebnikov combined futurist poetic form with the archaic imagery of pagan Russia. He attempted to create a meta-language of sounds and letters, and to decipher magic combinations of numbers that affect human history. In spite of his revolutionary inclinations, Khlebnikov's oeuvre was excluded from official literary anthologies because it was considered susceptible to undesirable interpretations. In homage, Bogdanov and Tchermensky have created a dense, multilayered environment to represent the complexity of the poet's vision. The museum interior, with its traditional domestic characteristics—parquet floor, mouldings on doors and windows, old-fashioned heating radiators—plays the role of the conventional world, fixed in historical time and space. Just as Khlebnikov's writings defied these stable referents in favor of a more complex view of existence, so the interior is populated with signs, marks, and fragments of other realities. The poet's thoughts and verses are scribbled directly on the walls; dynamic constructions, suspended in mid-air, recall his revolutionary aspirations. The density and eclecticism of the interior correspond to the spirit of Khlebnikov's limitless creativity.

Since 1988, Bogdanov and Tchermensky have been involved in a large-scale project for the Museum of the Russian-French Napoleonic War of 1812. For this project they have a chance to revise the entire

Velimir Khlebnikov Centennial Exhibition, Moscow, 1985, various views.

ПРОЛЕТАРИИ

museum space, including landscaping and outdoor exhibits. They will also participate in the selection of historical material, and even manufacture their own objects, including intricate figures of soldiers and horsemen. In the 1990s they should have many chances to employ their new aesthetic. In spite of the current political and economic crisis, a great many exhibitions are being organized. "The exhibitions serve as a safety-valve for culture," says Bogdanov. "When everything is being shattered, they restore our history." It appears that exhibiting is as important to the reformers of Russian society as it was to the officials of the totalitarian state. In spite of a radical reversal of values and goals, the paradigm of the Potemkin Village still exerts a powerful hold on the Russian imagination.

Left: Production Art exhibition, Moscow, 1984.

Production Art exhibition, Moscow,
1984, various views.

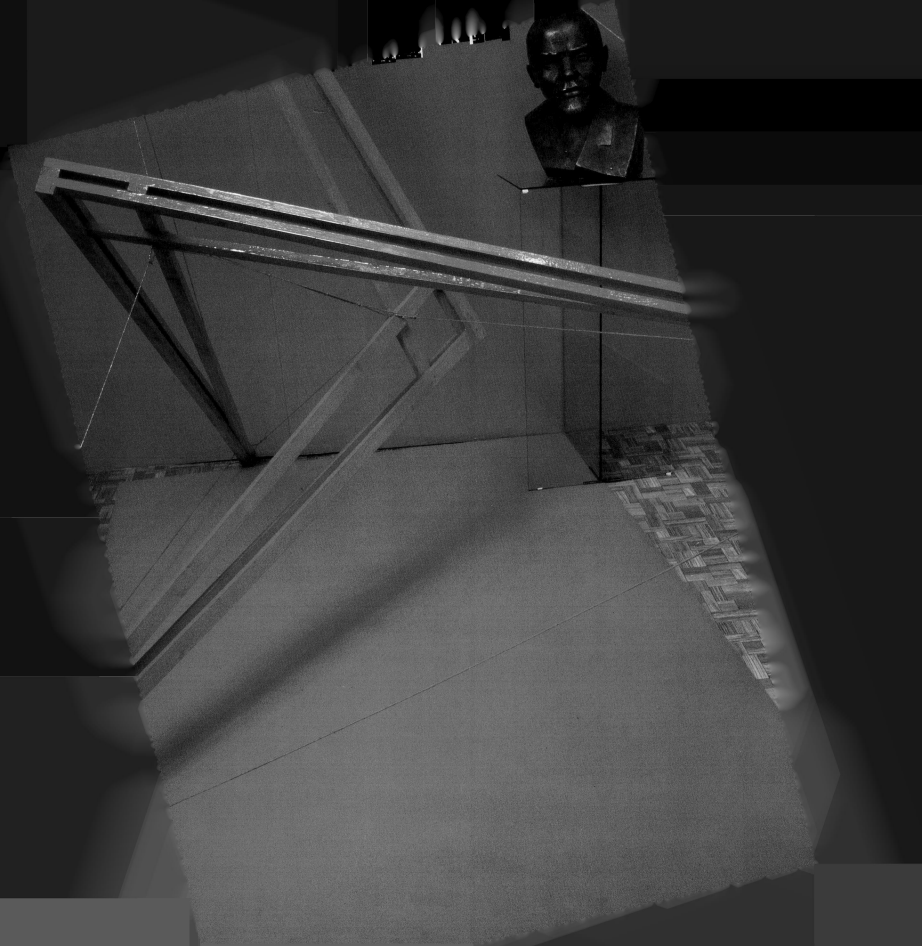

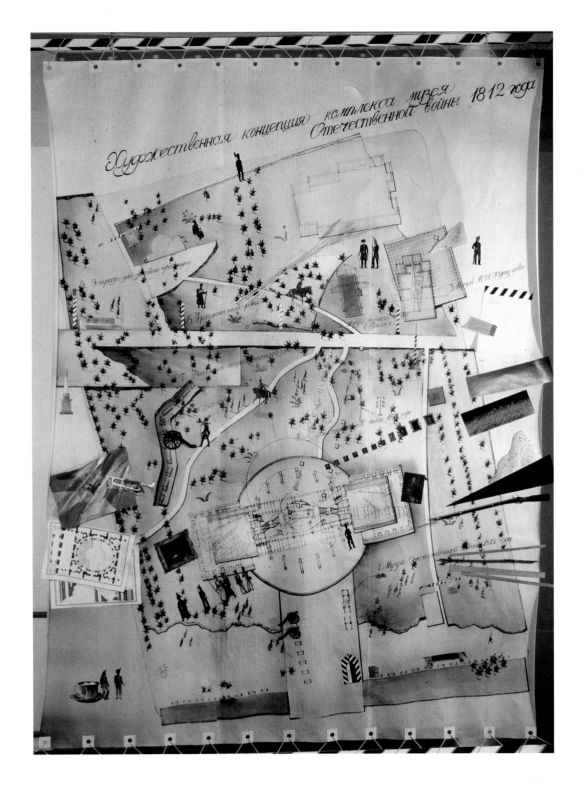

Above and above right: Permanent installation at the Museum of the Russian-French Napoleonic War of 1812, Moscow, 1988–90, model and master plan.

Industrial Design

DMITRY AZRIKAN

In his discussion of East European science fiction in the book *Art After Modernism,* Frederic Jameson also shows the surprising insight into the overall experience of Soviet life. He writes about "the radical strangeness and freshness of human existence and of its object world in a non-commodity atmosphere, in a space from which that prodigious saturation of messages, advertisements, and packaged libidinal fantasies of all kinds, is suddenly and unexpectedly stilled." A society devoid of consumerism, yet with shortages of the most elementary goods; filled with a great desire to "catch up with the West," yet with rudimentary trade and technical skills—what can possibly be the function of design in this environment?

When in the 1960s, design was introduced as part of the agenda of the state-run economy, this question was tackled by Soviet theorists. Understanding that Western design was a tool of the capitalist system, a means of conquering the market and creating extra profits for corporations, they looked at the specifics of Soviet design in a different light. "One doesn't care whether a machine is beautiful or not, if this machine remains an instrument of capitalist exploitation, and if a man is but its appendage," wrote Soviet critic Karl Kantor in 1967. "Our designers should always check their activity against this criterion: is it just a pretty object or is it a thing that establishes harmonious human relationships." Like most propaganda rhetoric, this statement had the appeal of a fairy tale, yet very little practical meaning. In fact, Soviet design from the start was put on an idealistic, utopian foundation. It seemed acceptable that designers at the central professional institute in Moscow (VNIITE) would work for years on esoteric

design programs, never to be implemented in the economic system. Not surprisingly, as the ideological foundations of totalitarian society crumbled in the late 1980s, the notion of industrial design, and the entire profession, appeared tainted with traces of the old Marxist-Leninist theoretical floridness.

Dmitry Azrikan has worked among design teams at VNIITE since the early years of the institute. In 1988 he became the first designer in the country to start his own independent studio. After so many years of creating theoretical, idealistic projects, one might expect pragmatism and common sense to be his new prevailing attitude. But the Azrikan Studio, located at the prestigious Arbat Square in Moscow, is still a bastion of utopian design. Now, however, Azrikan's goals and aspirations are directed away from "the truly socialist design" that occupied him and his colleagues for years. "We want commercial design, Western-style, to become a part of our life in Russia. We don't want to use found objects and 'poor' materials anymore. One cannot force people to live with 'poor design' when they dream about higher standards. This is our ethical stand," says Azrikan.

Azrikan's studio holds a privileged position in the Moscow professional design scene. Through the former patronage of the Union of Soviet Designers and exposure to foreign guests and companies, he has garnered considerable prestige. In spite of this, not many manufacturers are willing to commission design projects from him. Private enterprises are interested only in importation and selling, and state-run organizations have long lost any motivation for the development of new goods. One of the most fruitful collaborations has taken place with a television factory in Lvov. Interested in the exportation of its products abroad, the company decided to upgrade its assortment of television sets. The only type currently produced in the country is the ubiquitous box with wood-grain covering. Azrikan's proposals have

Above: Ice-cream maker, prototype.

included the *Structura* set, a structure that attempted to dispense with the encasing box, and the *Aqua* set, designed for the southern regions of the country. In the Caucasian and Middle-Asian republics of the south, people often watch television outside, on balconies, verandas, and in the gardens. Usually they cover the set with a piece of polyethylene film to protect it from rain and such. Azrikan's design has a watertight body with a pair of shutters for protection of the screen. When open, the shutters serve as speakers. There are three extendable legs as well, eliminating the need for boxes, bricks, or rocks to mount the set. The new designs were shocking to the clients, who were accustomed only to minor, decorative changes in the appearance of their products. Yet after some design modifications, the company is committed to developing the sets for production.

For a factory in Kiev, the Azrikan Studio developed an experimental version of a cable radio receiver. For decades such receivers have been a permanent fixture on the walls in every apartment in Russia, much like electrical outlets. In the totalitarian state, cable radio was considered more reliable and certainly more controllable than a wireless version. The image of this object, which had served as "the mouthpiece for the Big Brother," had to be radically changed, according to Azrikan. He designed it as a modular system with a distinct pattern of spherical elements. Optional additional elements, such as stereo speakers, could be attached, forming a continuous linear composition.

In one major project, Azrikan developed cashiers' workstations for Aeroflot, the state-owned air carrier, which held a virtual monopoly on all airline transportation in the country. "The airline counters, like many places in Russia where the public meets a state institution, have become the front lines of a war," comments Azrikan. Instead of traditional barriers and fences, the designers proposed a manifestation of openness—a workstation made entirely of tempered glass, with a large liquid crystal display, that allows the customer to see all booking data entered on computer. "The people in line always worry that something is being concealed from them. With this scheme they do not have to rely solely on the cashier's benevolence," Azrikan observes. Angular layout provides for a more personalized, individual client contact, compared to the traditional frontal linear counter.

Unfortunately, the chances for the implementation of projects such as this are not high. As the volume of local commissions plummets, an increasingly large part of the activity at the Azrikan Studio gets devoted to international competitions. Aside from an opportunity to earn much-needed hard currency, these projects serve as the perfect medium in which Azrikan can fantasize what Soviet design could be, had it all the necessary material and cultural resources. In 1990 the studio was successful in a competition for office systems, held by a Spanish company Galo/Ben; it shared a major prize with two other winners. The proposed office system was made out of dark-tinted triple glass, with printed circuits, digital clocks, and other information devices sandwiched between the glass layers. The technological and electronic complexity of the project, the sleekness of the dark glass and luxury of the marble inserts, clearly indicate the consumerist aesthetic preferences of Dmitry Azrikan and his colleagues. Like paupers in front of a glittering shop window, they look into a grandiose showcase of the world's commercial design, and they like what they see. If the stylistic features of the Azrikan Studio's work often betray a great deal of Western influence, its goal is both original and important for Russia: "We must keep the flame burning. Otherwise, the design profession will die out, and somebody will have to start again from nothing."

Above and right: Transformable
office chair, prototype, 1988,
standard and kneeling positions.

Opposite: Cashier's workstation for
Aeroflot, 1988–89.

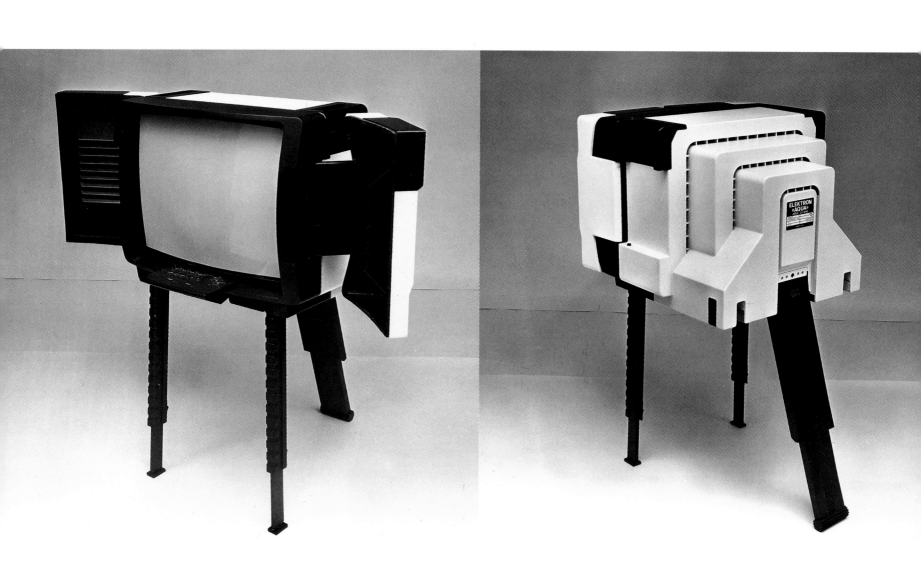

Above and above right: *Aqua*
outdoor television set for Electron,
1988–89.

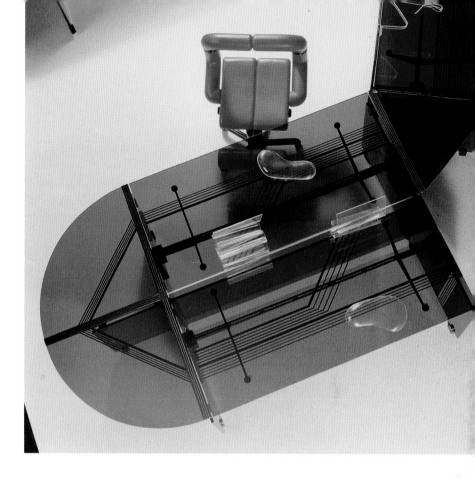

Office system, 1990, Prize of the
Jury in the Galo/Ben competition in
Spain, various views.

TATIANA SAMOILOVA

The great Russian writers of the nineteenth century, such as Dostoevsky and Chekhov, on the pages of their books passionately expressed the routine tragedy of "an insignificant human being"—one person's poverty, drudgery, and daily humiliation. Even though such characters were banished from the literature of Socialist Realism, the life of an average Soviet citizen was full of much of the same hopelessness. Although the October Revolution of 1917 from the outset claimed to be a movement of the masses, the first decrees of the nascent Soviet power already established an antagonism between collective and individual interests. "An individual had only two choices," observed Vladimir Paperny, "either to understand correctly the direction of the collective and to join in, or to understand it wrongly and to be crushed by the masses." Indeed, the historical developments of the 1930s—industrialization of the economy and collectivization of land—were conducted on a grandiose scale and with remarkable indifference to an individual's fate and suffering. Paradoxically, the "people's power" had very little concern with people's actual lives, their conditions of living and working, their comfort and welfare. Consumer products always remained a low priority in the centralized Soviet economy.

"They forgot about the human being," says designer Tatiana Samoilova of the former regime. For almost twenty years, she has fought to realize her humble earthly projects—small objects that relate to the human hand and address basic domestic needs. Samoilova studied at the Leningrad Artistic-Industrial School, where she graduated in 1962. Appropriately, given the country's design priorities at the time, she

spent the next ten years working in the Department of Heavy Machinery, designing tractors, trailers, and other utilitarian machines. By 1972, Tatiana well understood her own professional preferences. "I've found that I like working with objects that are close to people and that make their home environments beautiful," she says simply. Samoilova's programmatic stand is to work on mass-produced, inexpensive objects that can be handled and enjoyed by any person; a position of humanism, rarely discernible in Russian design.

Yet for almost fourteen years, not a single design of Samoilova's was put into production. Periodically, she was commissioned to develop a new product, but after several bureaucratic delays the project would inevitably get shelved. Noticeable changes first took place in 1986. The renewed economic climate of the early years of perestroika stimulated two factories in the Ukraine to start production of Samoilova's objects for the mass market. In the course of the following years she saw, incredulously, her electric razors, watches, a miniature sewing machine, lighters, and manicure sets all appearing in department stores.

The rounded, organic shapes of Samoilova's designs emphasize her interest in the ergonomic, utilitarian aspects of an object put into daily use. She always utilizes standard mechanical parts and existing tools and technologies; without this approach, no factory would even attempt production. Yet the playful, colorful character of her works places them apart from the typically bland consumer items one finds in Russia. Essentially, Samoilova's objects are rare Russian examples of "toys for adults": they are products bought and appreciated not only for their usefulness, but for the visual and tactile pleasure that they offer. It is difficult to discern specifically Russian features, or any personal idiosyncrasies, in the design language of Samoilova. She firmly believes that "design is international." Accordingly, her influences

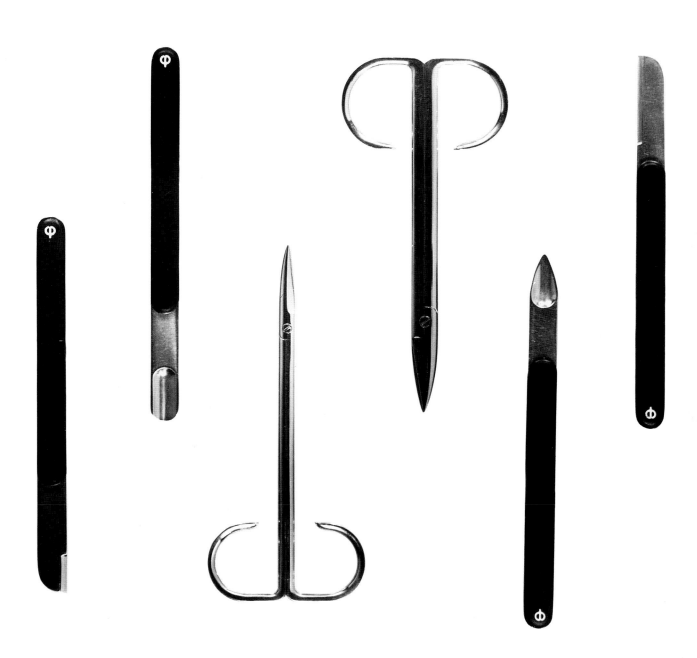

Above: Manicure set.

Below: Manicure set.

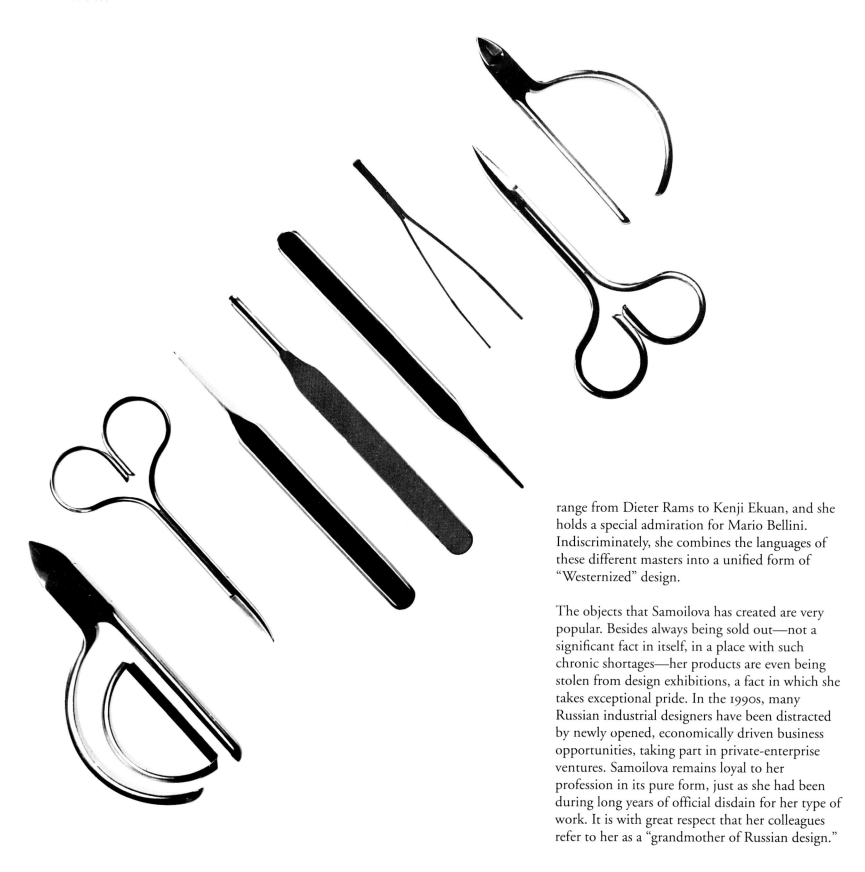

range from Dieter Rams to Kenji Ekuan, and she holds a special admiration for Mario Bellini. Indiscriminately, she combines the languages of these different masters into a unified form of "Westernized" design.

The objects that Samoilova has created are very popular. Besides always being sold out—not a significant fact in itself, in a place with such chronic shortages—her products are even being stolen from design exhibitions, a fact in which she takes exceptional pride. In the 1990s, many Russian industrial designers have been distracted by newly opened, economically driven business opportunities, taking part in private-enterprise ventures. Samoilova remains loyal to her profession in its pure form, just as she had been during long years of official disdain for her type of work. It is with great respect that her colleagues refer to her as a "grandmother of Russian design."

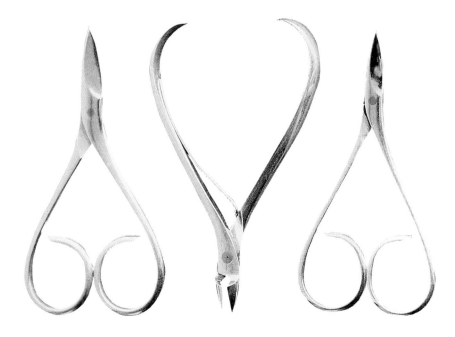

Top: Wristwatches, prototypes.

Above: Manicure set.

Right: Scissors (in collaboration with I. Chuprun).

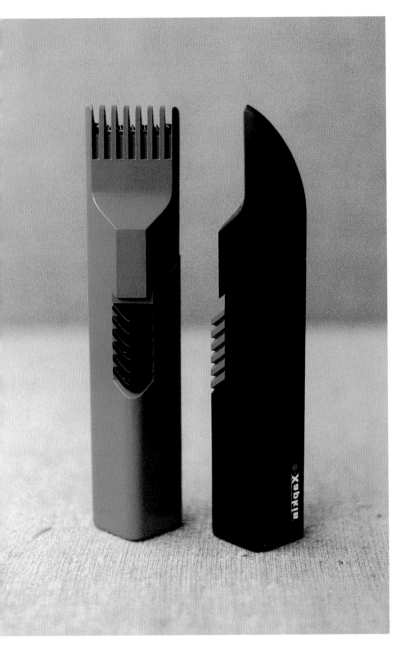

Above: Electric razor (in collaboration with I. Chuprun).

Above left: Hair trimmer (in collaboration with I. Chuprun).

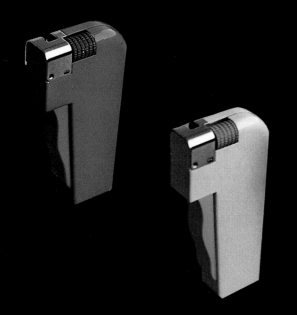

Above: Wristwatches (in collaboration with S. Pashkovskaya).

Right: Heater (in collaboration with I. Chuprun).

Below right: Sewing machine (in collaboration with E. Mongayt).

Below left: Hair trimmer (in collaboration with I. Chuprun).

Left: Lighter (in collaboration with I. Chuprun).

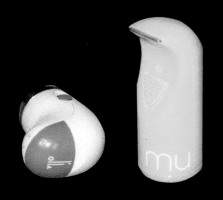

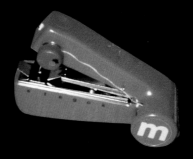

VLADIMIR TELYAKOV

Theater assumed a great importance in the cultural life of postrevolutionary Russia of the 1920s. For artists it became a laboratory in which to test their creative concepts. The Soviet government generally approved of experimental theater, seeing it as a forum for political education. To the people, public

performances and mass spectacles provided a new kind of entertainment, where familiar forms of carnivals and religion-based events were imbued with contemporary content. The theater of the 1920s proved to be one of the most vital revolutionary art forms, a unifying force that combined the efforts of virtually every major figure of the Russian avant-garde.

Vladimir Telyakov grew up inspired by the integrating power of the theater. Born in 1948, Telyakov came to design in an unusual way, having received a degree in engineering from a radio-technological institute. He then studied design at the Stroganoff Art School. Upon graduation in 1975, Telyakov was employed by a research institute where he developed electronic components and audio appliances. Typically for Soviet industry of the time, most of his projects were getting shelved, or at best being materialized as working prototypes. Telyakov began looking for a way to demonstrate the possibilities of newly designed objects, to prove that they could be integrated into the Soviet people's lifestyle. By the early 1980s, he had organized an experimental group that became known as Design Theater.

"The cultural connection between design and other arts has fallen apart," says Telyakov. "Only when artists in different fields—designers, craftsmen, fashion stylists, painters, actors, musicians, and so

on—start working together will the design process achieve wholeness and richness." The performances of Design Theater aspired to such integration. The group's work focused on the human interaction with design. Each show combined music, theater, mime, fashion, and objects, which were often carried or worn by characters. The conventional relationship between props and actors was turned on its head; the accessories became the true protagonists of the show, rather than elements of a decorative setting. Objects were considered from emotional, intellectual, and other perspectives, each characterized by a particular design language.

Telyakov's own design direction evolved from a synthesis of these aesthetic impulses. On a theoretical level, he was intrigued by the concept of integrating natural and mechanical organs, of concentrating and expanding human sensations and abilities. His sketches show humanoid faces almost completely covered by electrical and mechanical devices. "What is it about this fabled creature, the cyborg, that has so captured the popular imagination?" wrote journalist Steve Beard when *Terminator 2* hit movie screens around the world. "Part of the answer is that the cyborg offers up a fantasy of absolute self-sufficiency in a time of general social collapse and escalating panic." Perhaps Telyakov's fascination with the man-machine also originated as a sublimation of his effort to confront the inhuman and impersonal routine of totalitarian society.

Telyakov's *Futurological Objects* (some of them are working prototypes) continue the theme of fusing natural and mechanical elements, and raising the results to a sophisticated artistic level. His schemes for headphone sets have a high degree of technological complexity; they include a telephone and radio and connect to a central computer network. The sensory aspects of these objects are also unusual. For example, his proposed metal bracelets function as hand

Above: Cassette player for the
Tsyklon research institute, 1982.

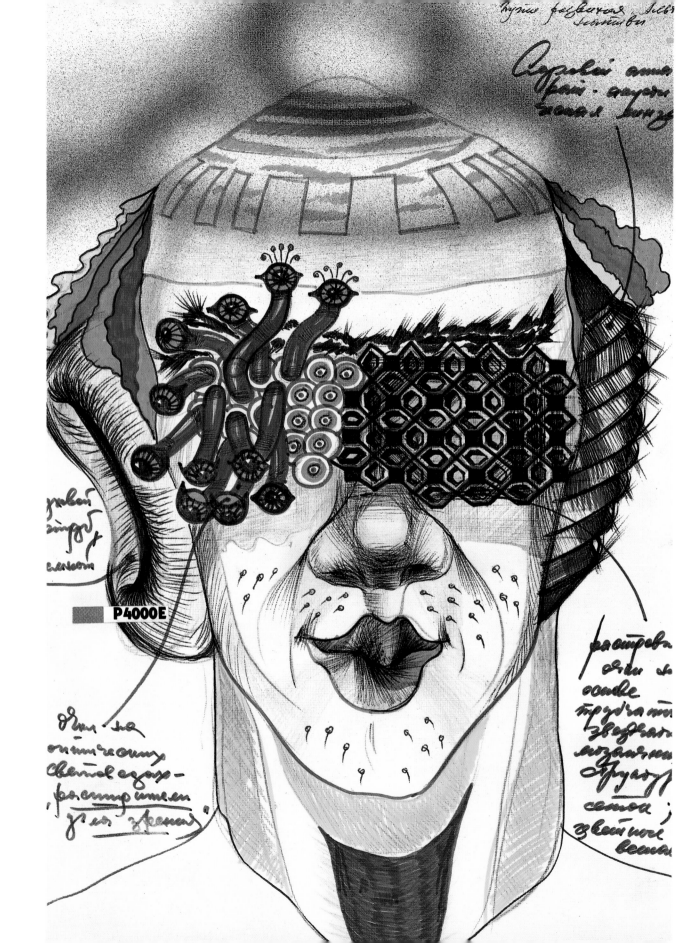

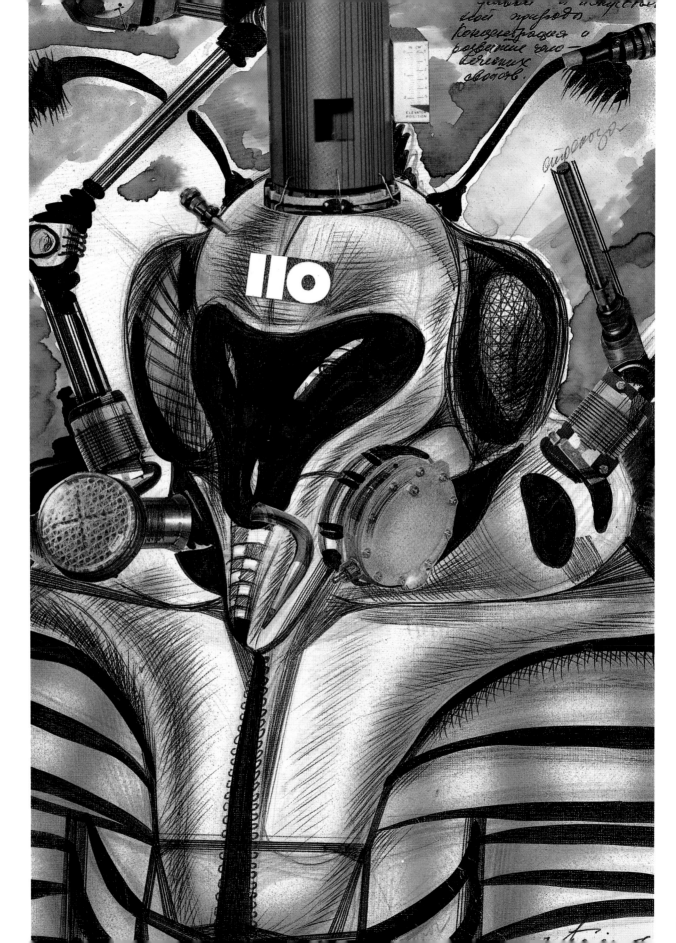

Right and opposite: *Man-Machine concept*, 1987, sketches.

Above: Automatic record player for the
Tsyklon research institute, 1980.

thermostats that heat the hand in cold weather and
cool it in summer. Eyeglasses are designed to broaden
visual perception, and they have a special attachment
for the bridge of the nose in order to intensify smells.
The hard look of industrial design objects is also
applied to women's bags, purses, and jewelry, which
are composed of electronic and mechanical
components. The pieces are never photographed on a
neutral background; in the spirit of Design Theater,
they are worn by models—held by a hand or hung
from the body.

The design language of Telyakov's objects is heavily
influenced by the look of the Soviet military equipment; he grew familiar with those instruments from
his work at a research institute. The popular belief
has long regarded military technology as the most
dependable and efficient aspect of the Soviet econo-
political system. Telyakov was the first to appreciate
the aesthetic appeal of this technology—its powerful,
rugged forms, its characteristic khaki color. The
designer then willfully merged the munitions aesthetic with the liberating elements of 1970s Italian design,
borrowed from the pages of *Domus* magazines. Intu-

itively, Telyakov picked up the anthropological
dimension of the New Italian design. In the words of
Alessandro Mendini, such an approach "places a man
at the core of any environmental activity, starting
from the body and going on to cosmetics, clothes,
rooms, decor, the city." Similarly, the Design Theater
of Vladimir Telyakov regards technology, products,
and fashion as expressive extensions of the five basic
bodily senses.

Telyakov's inquiries are especially remarkable in a
country that until recently had been virtually devoid
of consumer electronics. The radical nature of his
design proposals prevented them from being
materialized on the Soviet assembly lines. As the
market opens up in the 1990s, there appears an
obstacle of a different nature: a flow of cheap Western
appliances, instantly sold out in Russian stores. The
body of Telyakov's work—visionary design
understood as a cultural mission—does not offer
itself to easy industrial realization, neither in
technological nor in commercial terms. Telyakov has
found that it is hard to sell "theater props," even if
they are the protagonists of the show.

Futurological Objects, 1983–89.
Above: Shortwave radio; right, top
and bottom: shortwave radio for
the beach; left: headphone radio.

Futurological Objects, 1983–89.
Top: Headphone radio with
telephone and computer
connection, and hand thermostat-
bracelets; above: woman's purse;
right: techno-jewelry.

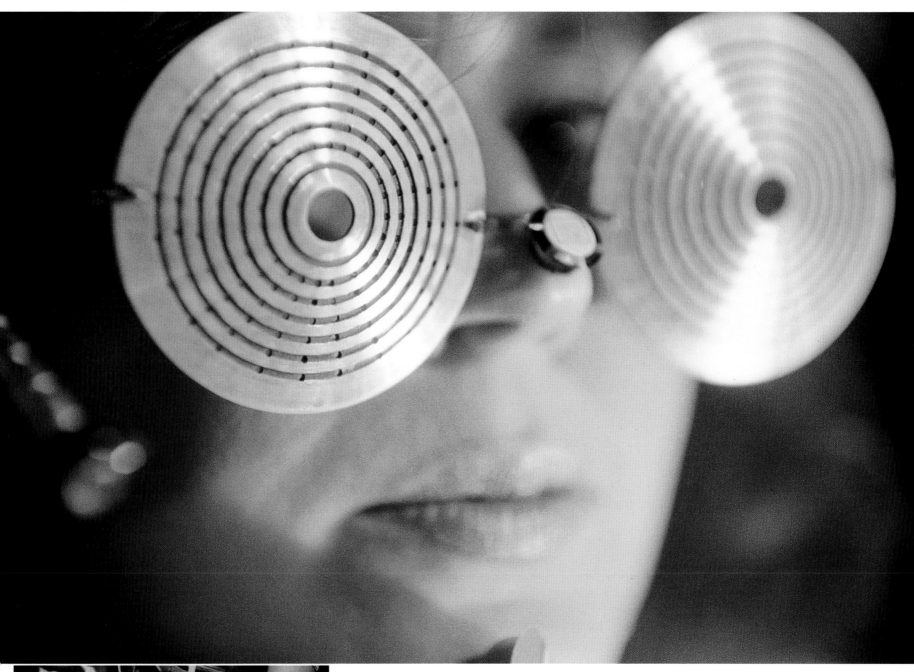

Futurological Objects, 1983–89.
Above: Raster sunglasses with
sensory attachment for smell
intensification; far left: woman's
purse; near left: shoulder bag.

LEONID YENTUS

When Brezhnev's Soviet Union reluctantly signed an International Accord on Human Rights in 1973, a tiny crack in the Iron Curtain opened up for a small portion of the Soviet population. According to one of the Accord stipulations, a limited number of Jewish families were allowed to emigrate from the Soviet Union to reunite with their relatives in Israel. In spite of the law, emigration was never made easy. People who sought it were banned from work, ostracized, harassed, and then waited for years for permission to leave. Those who were refused remained blacklisted forever. Still, the number of applicants grew every year, until the flow was finally stopped in 1981. With Gorbachev's liberating reforms, emigration again became an option for Soviet Jews, and many chose the uncertainty of the promised land over the domestic promises of the Communist Party leader.

Moscow designer Leonid Yentus waited until the end of 1989 to seek permission to emigrate. After a number of years, he had given up on Russia as a place to realize his goals. "As a provincial boy, I came to Moscow trying to achieve something in design. I failed," says Yentus. "But I wonder, was it also the capital that failed?" Born in 1945 in the southern city of Odessa, Yentus started his studies there, then continued in Leningrad. He eventually graduated from Moscow's Stroganoff Art School in 1974. He devoted the next ten years of his professional life to work at KDOI, the state agency of decorative arts, designing museum exhibitions and installations. In the oppressive atmosphere of the 1970s, he found an inner meaning in working with museums, dealing with history and art, reinterpreting the cultural heritage.

In 1977 Yentus was one of the key members in the first "independent" exhibition featuring young Moscow designers. The group show attempted to establish its own creative direction, distancing itself both from the design institution of VNIITE, and

from the craft excesses of the Senezh studio. The furniture that Yentus presented at the exhibition was characteristic of the whole show: soft, flexible, and modular, fashioned from flat fabric bags tied together with rope. He and his fellow designers glorified raw, amateur creativity, asserting the humanist spirit of a hand-made, personalized environment. In the conditions of the time, however, these proposals could assume only a symbolic value: such was the position of many critics who approvingly but cautiously reviewed the show.

An opportunity for a realizable design project came to Yentus around 1985. He was contacted by Soyuztheaprom, a company that had developed electro-mechanical theater props, toys, and game machines. Usually, the company had no need for a designer: antiquated foreign machines were routinely purchased, dismantled, then reproduced with simplifications by in-house engineers. This time, the directors wanted something different. They asked Yentus to come up with a new concept for "good" games, as opposed to the avaricious ones of the capitalist West. Curiously, the game machines were to be produced by a military factory that, according to a new regulation, had to devote up to three percent of its volume to consumer-oriented products.

Perhaps a game machine could help develop a child's perception, thought Yentus. He envisioned a device that connected color with musical sound. The Russian composer Scriabin had experimented with color-music at the beginning of the twentieth century; the pulsating lighting design in discos shows that the

Color-Music Game Machine for Soyuztheaprom, 1985. Top: First proposal; above and right: final proposals.

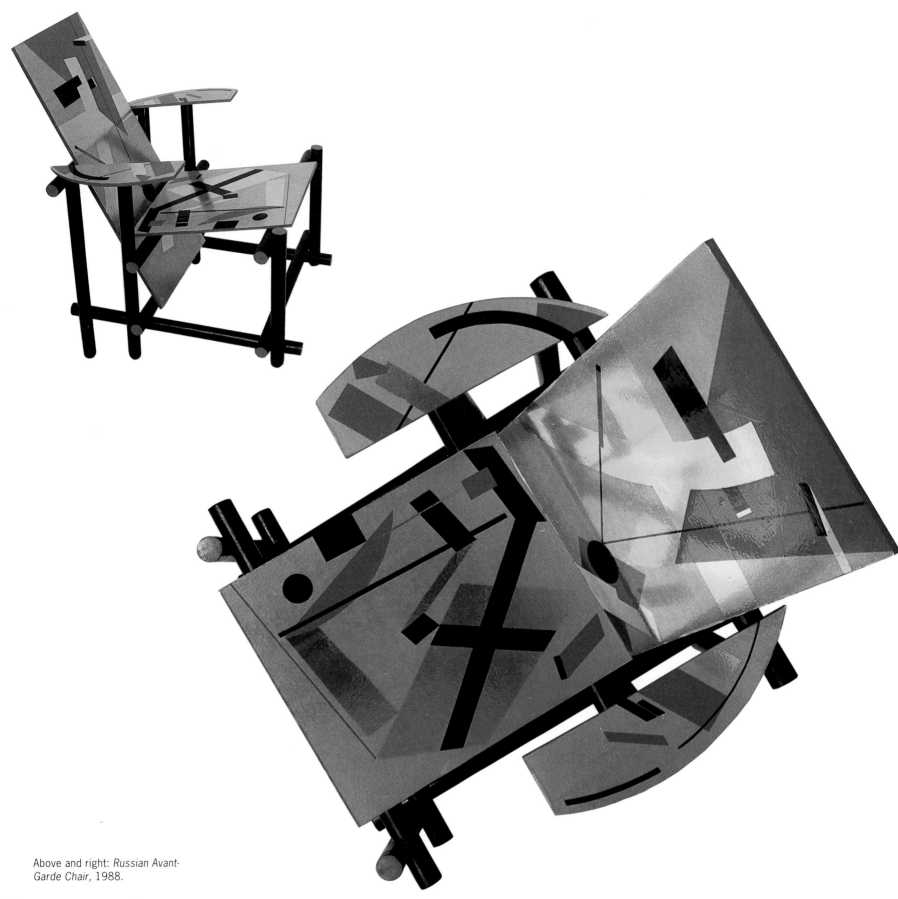

Above and right: *Russian Avant-Garde Chair*, 1988.

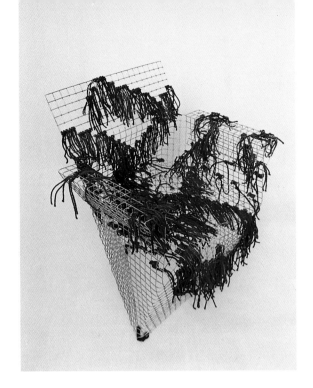

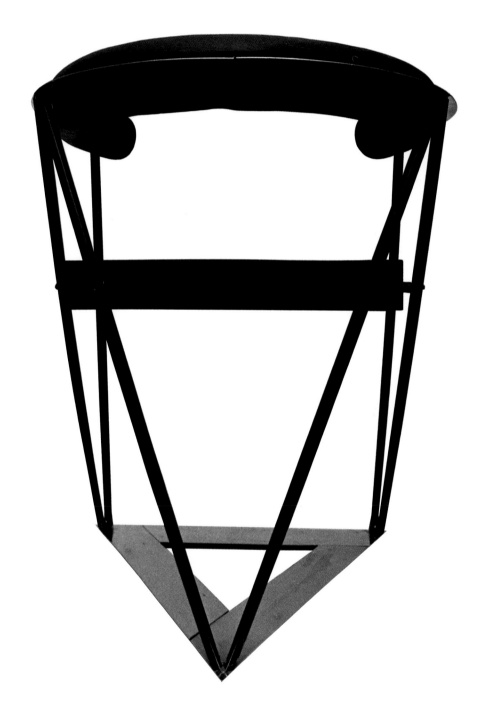

Top: *Green Chair*, 1988.

Above and above right: *Magic
Chair*, 1989.

Right: Furniture from the Young Moscow Designers exhibition, 1977.

idea has never lost its appeal. In a bold gesture, Yentus juxtaposed the grimness of military equipment with the glamour of a symphony orchestra. Flutes and trombones literally grew out of the ends of rifles and machine guns in his first design proposal. "I wanted to channel a military aggressiveness into a different outlet, to turn it into a creative impulse," explains the designer. Even though a revised version of his thoughtful project was accepted by the client, the factory had neither the economic motivation nor technical expertise to put it in production.

In 1988 Yentus started his series of "chairs-posters." *The Russian Avant-Garde Chair* originated as an entry to a competition held by the Artists' Union. Yentus designed it as a series of oppositions, combined into "the difficult whole" of a collage. The chair derives from a Western prototype—Rietveld's iconic *Red and Blue Chair*—yet it is made out of spade handles, a distinctly Russian material. Yentus uses the Constructivist compositions of El Lissitzky as decoration, yet the overall painting technique imitates an Old Russian craft, rich with gold glimmer. *The Green Chair* is devoted to the emerging Green movement in the Soviet Union. It is folded, origami-like, from a single sheet of flexible steel netting. In the spirit of the Greens, the structure is held together only with multiple ties of cotton rope. Green tapestry, like ivy, covers parts of this surprisingly sturdy and comfortable chair.

Perhaps the most intriguing aspect of Yentus's chairs is the way they oppose their expressive, art-furniture appearance with a pragmatic, economical construction technique. Reading about the achievements of the new Italian design, Yentus dreamed of limited-edition production of his own furniture. He figured

if he could make objects with his own bare hands, then small private enterprises could undertake production of them as well. By 1988, privately owned cooperative businesses were legalized by the Soviet government as a means of boosting a sluggish economy. Yentus invited a number of cooperative businessmen to his studio to show them his work. No pieces went into production, however, as the businessmen realized that furniture manufacturing was not a quick or profitable enough way to earn the income they desired.

The designer's frustration is reflected in *Nomenclatura Chair*, one of the last of his projects completed in Russia. This grotesque chair recalls the extravagances of Soviet architecture and of the kitschy aesthetics of bureaucracy. The monumental, symmetrical front of the chair is covered with faux-marble paint and counterbalanced with almost invisible back legs made of ski poles. The seat is made of fake Astrakhan fur, a status symbol of the Soviet elite. But it is not enough for him to make a statement. "I am not interested in a pure metaphor," says Yentus. "The chair has to be structurally and technologically sound: it has to be a piece of design."

Since moving to New York, Yentus has begun working for Gaetano Pesce, an Italian designer famous for his hands-on furniture techniques and idiosyncratic treatment of materials. Pesce's studio, an amalgam of a medieval sweatshop and a creative laboratory, is Yentus's first exposure to Western design practices. The son of a metalsmith and grandson of a tailor, he knows the necessity and value of apprenticeship. At forty-six, he has started his professional career anew, an experience that every Russian emigré will always remember.

Above and above right:
Nomenclatura Chair, 1989.

Graphic Design

Opposite: Cover design of *Reklama* magazine, 1990.

VLADIMIR CHAIKA

The policy of glasnost was a difficult blessing for Russia. Besides opening to the public long-suppressed information about the past, glasnost also exposed an abyss of the present: a corrupt, backward, hopelessly mismanaged economy, with no clear direction for the future. Conscientious professionals in many creative fields found themselves in a state of crisis. How could, say, a graphic designer continue to make up sleek graphic programs for backward industrial complexes or for hypocritical public organizations? Besides, as the centralized government system weakened, no continuous flow of work was directed to designers' offices. Out of this unpromising environment emerged the talent of Vladimir Chaika.

Chaika was born in 1955 and spent the first twelve years of his life in Kazakhstan, where his father served as an officer at a military base. He then studied at the Stroganoff Art School in Moscow, specializing in graphic design. He was still a student when he was first offered a job at Promgraphika, a prestigious state-run studio. There he participated in the development of large-scale, unimaginative graphic programs so representative of the late Brezhnev period. These projects brought the young designer professional recognition, awards, and a clearly promising future. He was close to becoming an executive art director of the entire studio.

At that time glasnost had already drawn a curtain back from the country's history, and many previously forbidden literary and historical texts became accessible to the public. Books such as *The Gulag*

Archipelago had a profound influence on Chaika. Once a loyal Communist, he left his position at the studio, cancelled many previous assignments and contracts, and in an unprecedented gesture for 1987, abandoned his Communist Party membership. "I got sick and tired of lying," recalls Chaika. "Tired of superficial projects that nobody really needed, that burst like soap bubbles at the first touch with the reality of our life." He shaved his head, as a sign of mourning, and as a farewell to the trendy-designer stereotype.

During a year-long period of crisis, Chaika formulated his new direction. In a stationery store he bought some black ink, small sheets of plain paper, and a children's glue brush with which to work. This was his "technological base," appropriate for the country in which he was working, and it helped him to form a new design language. In fact, he calls it an "anti-language," a rough and defiant utilization of the most primitive, throw-away materials. A virtuoso of calligraphy, Chaika chose to scribble with a glue brush in order to imitate the casualness of amateur expression. And he became particularly discriminating with his choice of clients. "I was going to do only the projects for which there was a real need, only those where I could help somebody," he recalls.

For all their undesigned roughness, Chaika's new projects stood out thanks to their strong conceptual bent, a visual and metaphorical key that immediately captured one's attention. For a 1988 Moscow exhibition, "Designer-Artist," organized jointly by VNIITE and by the Union of Soviet Artists, Chaika created a four-part poster that captured the tenuous relationship between the two disciplines. The first sheet depicts a French curve, a symbol and a tool for designers. In the subsequent sheets, the tool is progressively shattered, with its pieces forming an abstract composition. As parts of the poster were

ISSN 0132—5604

№ 5

РЕКЛАМА

90

TRADEMARK

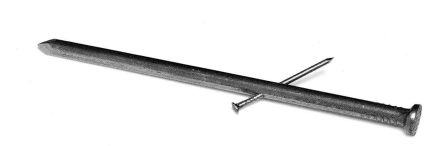

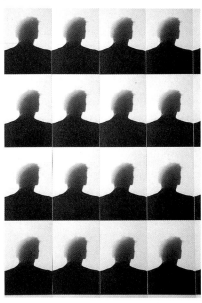

posted around the city, the order of reading could vary from centrifugal to centripetal. One could interpret it as a design product that disintegrates into a work of art, or conversely, as an abstract piece forming a figurative functional object. In another project for an exhibition, entitled *A Debate on the Beauty,* Chaika played with foreground and background to create a work with a double reading. Depending on one's point of view, the image appeared either as two profiles (a debate) or as a classical vase (beauty).

One of Chaika's most memorable and frustrating experiences was his work for the Society of Victims of Stalinist Repressions (Memorial), established in 1989. First Chaika participated in a competition for the society's graphic identity program, and won the top prize with an expressive, very rough entry that effectively subverted the very idea of corporate identity. Later in 1990, he took part in a contest for a monument to the victims. This competition, open to any citizen of the USSR, drew several thousand entries. Chaika proposed a very long wall, somewhere in Siberia, with over thirty million heads, one for each victim, executed in ceramic bas-relief. The startling rationalist precision of the project brought Chaika another first prize. Yet both his proposals were immediately shelved. The ethical dimension of Chaika's design work—his desire to help people—has proven to be harder to express than it has been for him to win competitions.

One of the champions of Chaika's work has been *Reklama* magazine. After Vasily Tsygankov took over as art director in 1983, the publication became an important showcase of Soviet graphic design. Since 1984, Chaika designed more than twenty memorable covers for the magazine. His farewell cover of 1990 coincided with his departure for America, at the special invitation of the New York designers Massimo and Lella Vignelli. In the trademark style of the Coca-Cola logo, the copy reads, *"Piva Net"* (Beer is Sold Out)—a sign familiar to every Russian who has stood in long lines waiting for a beer—a sad symbol of the country's material deficiencies. Despite his long-awaited departure, the consumer paradise of the West left Chaika surprised, confused, and ultimately, alienated. He could not fathom the creative and monetary resources expended for something that would end up as junk mail. While appreciating the strength and precision of American graphic design, he instinctively sensed its lack of a spiritual core. His idealism did not find acceptance in the pragmatic New York design scene, just as his whole-hearted openness seemed awkward amid the polite smiles of indifference.

Chaika has returned to Moscow, with no clear direction of which way to go. In a small studio apartment, where he lives with his wife and young son, he works at a kitchen table, making ambiguous, grotesque, unsettling compositions and objects. These untitled works are his personal reflections, glimpses into personal anxieties, as he perhaps hopes for a return to the graphic design profession. With a charming smile he quotes Solzhenitsyn: "'Don't trust, don't beg, don't fear!' This was the man's motto in a Gulag camp. Appropriate for all of us here, isn't it?"

Below: Re-design of the standard graphics (bottom) on the Kazbek cigarette box.

Above, left, center, and right: Four-part poster for the Designer-Artist Exhibition, Moscow, 1988, posters 2, 3, and 4.

Below, left, center, and right: Eighteenth Exhibition of Young Moscow Artists (*A Debate on the Beauty*), Moscow, 1988, poster, invitation, and three-dimensional decorative element.

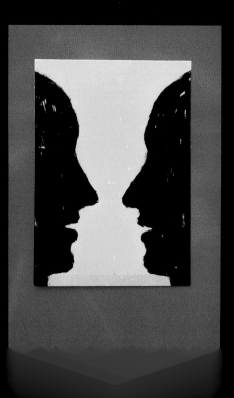

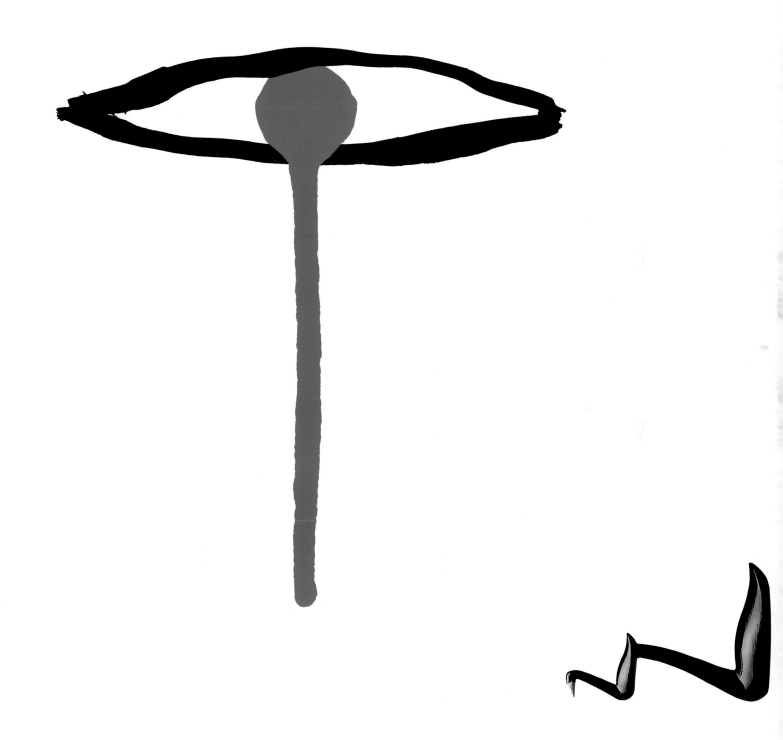

Above: *Untitled*, 1991.

Right: *Swan Lake*, toy, prototype.

Above: Logo of the Green
Movement in Russia, 1991.

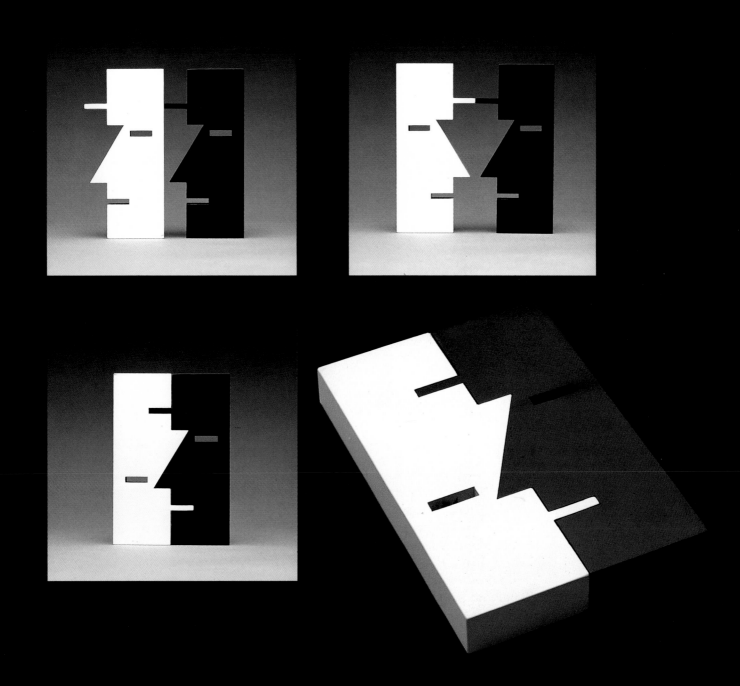

Above: *Cometogether*, toy,
prototype.

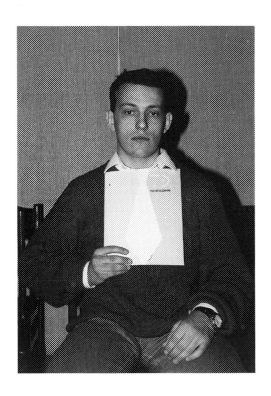

ALEXANDER GELMAN

After the many years of Socialist Realism's reign, graphic design in Russia has largely remained dependent on pictorial imagery and narrative content. Soviet graphics of the 1970s aspired to create direct and minimal systems of visual communications, based on Swiss-style examples, but were infused with the realistic heritage of the previous decades. Even a series of pictograms for the Moscow Olympics in 1980, for example, emphasized recognizable mimetic silhouettes over the abstract logic of coded visual information.

It takes, therefore, a lot of confidence for twenty-four-year-old Alexander Gelman to formulate as his design credo, "I don't depict anything, as a matter of principle." Gelman graduated from the 1905 Art School in 1987, where he studied environmental design. His training helped Alexander to formulate an ambitious design program that he follows almost fanatically. Gelman aspires to go beyond two-dimensionality of graphic design. "I want to break the rules of the genre, to turn flat sheets of paper into a spatial show, and to invite everyone to participate in the design act," he explains. Remarkably, Gelman often manages to achieve his goal, working for clients on real-life assignments.

Thus, he designed a program for a concert by Van Cliburn at the Moscow Conservatory in an oversized folded format. As more of these subtly colored programs were being opened up in the concert hall, the audience appeared to be dressed up in color-coordinated costumes. The concert program did indeed venture into three-dimensional space, becoming a fan, a wearable decorative screen, and a holiday baton.

In 1989, Gelman was entrusted with a plum job: to create a series of covers for *TE* (Technical Esthetics) magazine, an official periodical of Soviet industrial

design. Again, Gelman sought to destroy the traditional flatness of a magazine cover. In some of his illustrations he uses illusionist tricks, suggesting an open door or a ladder with a cast shadow, done in a restrained, semiabstract way. One issue of *TE,* devoted to car design, features the stretched word "auto," in a type commonly used for road marking. The word only becomes readable if one tilts the magazine at a particular angle, approximating a driver's view of the road. Does this demand too much from the reader? "Since I had an opportunity to do a whole series of covers, I wanted to build up a certain expectation," says Gelman. "One after another, these covers offer unexpected solutions, helping to cultivate the subscribers' design taste."

Such design education, for Gelman, should take a populist stand, embracing humor, narrative scenarios, and public participation. Thus, one copy of *TE* got decorated with circular traces of plates and coffee mugs. "It was an invitation to use the magazine actively: to have breakfast with it, to feel free putting it under your coffee," he explains. Another example of Gelman's "active use" occurred in an issue devoted to color in fashion and product design. A geometric outline of a necktie was accompanied with a brief, ambiguous note: "See page 16." On that page, the text read: "Color is a major factor in a fashionable suit, and a tie is the final touch. Our tie on the cover, however, is white. We invite you to fill it with color and to send the cover back to the editors." This proposition, which might be suitable for a children's magazine, looked shocking and daring in a sober, mostly black-and-white professional publication.

Gelman produces his work with a surprising economy of means. He never uses more than two colors, because the risk of distortion at Soviet printing presses is too great. The type, lines, and shapes of his graphic solutions are always blocky and rectangular, as if industrially fabricated. He prefers

ISSN 0136—5363

№10(322)1990

CM. C. 13—16.

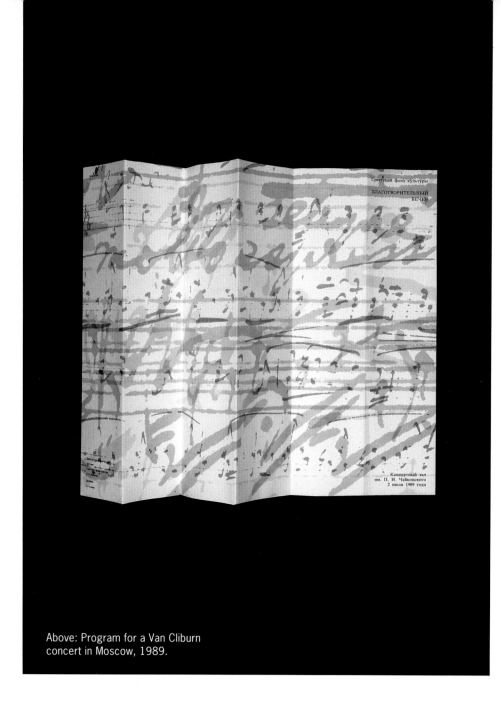

Above: Program for a Van Cliburn
concert in Moscow, 1989.

design that combines an impoverished look with an
elegance of concept. In creating a logo for a
documentary film studio called *Nerv* (nerve), Gelman
used the shape of the common Russian razor blade
called *Neva*. The simple substitution of a couple of
letters created a powerful logo and an unexpected
semantic connection between word and object.
Gelman's logo for VNIITE also suggests creative
economy: it can be stretched as necessary in order to
serve a variety of uses, from business cards and
stationery to filling up a required advertising space.

Gelman's use of industrial language, an economy
of means and materials, and his aspiration to
participatory action relates his graphic design work
to Constructivist methodology. Unlike many of his
compatriots, he manages to avoid what Hal Foster
called "fetishistic Constructivism": a postmodernist
simulation of the 1920s aesthetics, divorced from its
critical analysis and ideological basis. Gelman's
position is ethical rather than aesthetic. He refuses
to please the eye alone, just as earlier he refuted a
conventional and superfluous system of official
graphics. New methods, harsh and direct, should
bring design back to reality, he believes. In 1989, in
a bold attempt to combine graphics with body
language, Gelman made a series of photographic
autoportraits, entitled *False Clarity*. One of these
made it to the cover of *Reklama* magazine; it shows
Gelman attempting to open his shut eyes, only to
reveal a painted sign gaping at the viewer. The cover
calls on designers to tear the blinders off their eyes,
to liberate their vision, to face reality directly and
urgently. Gelman is not afraid of creative
competition.

ISSN 0136–5363

№7(319)1990

№9(321)1990

Above and right: Cover designs, *TE*
magazine, 1990.

BHUUME

BHUUME

Above and right: Logo for VNIITE
(Research Institute of Technical
Esthetics), 1989. The logo can be
stretched as necessary for
different applications.

Above: Logo for Nerv
documentary film studio, 1990.

Right: Cover design, *TE*
magazine, 1990.

№8(320)1990

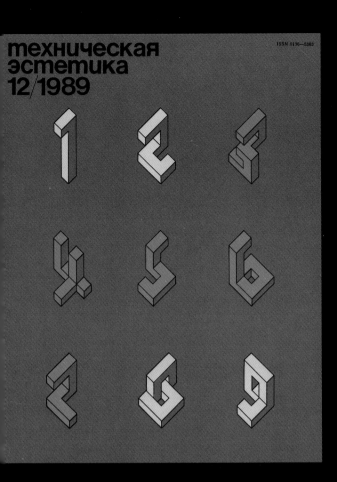

Above: Cover design, *TE* magazine, 1989, with three-dimensional typeface.

Above right: Logo for Otechestvo (Fatherland) Publishers, 1989.

Right: New Year's Card, 1989.

№6

РЕКЛАМА

'89

ISSN 0132-5604

НА ПОЛИТИЧЕСКУЮ РЕКЛАМУ
ПОКА СМОТРЯТ С НАСТОРОЖЕННОСТЬЮ.
НЕ ПРИШЛА ЛИ ПОРА УЗАКОНИТЬ ЕЕ В ПРАВАХ!

Right: *False Clarity*, cover design,
Reklama magazine, 1989

IGOR BEREZOVSKY

Among the sculptural gifts that the governments of different countries have presented to the United Nations Headquarters in New York, there are two Soviet sculptural compositions. One, installed in 1959, shows a muscular male who reshapes a sword into a plowshare; the other, realized in 1990, portrays St. George slaying a dragon made of nuclear missiles. Both of these works demonstrate one of the most pervasive Russian cultural forms: the didactic, verbalist allegory. From the 1930s on, this literary category has penetrated architecture and art as well; it has conditioned the perception of any artistic act, even most progressive conceptual endeavors in the time of perestroika.

Igor Berezovsky has shunned the rhetoric of allegories and metaphors since the beginning of his career. Born in 1941, he did not have formal training in design. In 1967, after a period of apprenticeship at several art and photo studios, he joined the graphic design group at the recently organized VNIITE. It was a brief euphoric time for Soviet design, when the young believed they could make a difference, thinking that a focused artistic effort could somehow improve the country's sad economic and cultural state of affairs. Berezovsky envisioned the discipline of graphic design as an example of pure visual culture—a new and atypical model for a country long indoctrinated by the verbalism of Socialist Realism. He was deeply affected by the powerful artistic statement of Pop Art, which he had seen in reproductions on the pages of foreign magazines. Without knowing the sources and social meanings of these images, he was attracted by the new technological means of generating artworks, through the combined use of photography, silk screening, and acrylic paint. Berezovsky felt that a similar approach could liberate him and lead him to new modes of visual expression. He and his colleagues experimented with photographs, enlarging, solarizing, tinting and superimposing them.

For the graphic program of the Ninth Congress of ICSID in Moscow in 1975, he used the visual image of a crowd, so characteristic of the early Russian avant-garde. The image, drawn from a documentary photograph, was manipulated so that enlarged or reduced fragments of it could appear on the Congress's posters, stationery, and signage. Berezovsky planned to use simple two-color printing and cheap paper for the program, considering it futile to compete with the West in terms of luxury and printing quality. The directors of VNIITE, however, found this "poor design" politically incorrect and not representative; the project was fundamentally changed and reduced in scope.

More and more Berezovsky came under artistic and bureaucratic pressure. His poster for an exhibition of Soviet design in Stuttgart was published only after much fighting and delay. The degree of geometrical abstraction and immaterial thinness in Berezovsky's hammer and sickle, the state symbol, looked subversive to the officials of Soviet culture.

Berezovsky left VNIITE in 1976, disillusioned with the institute and frustrated with the design profession. "Graphic design is supposed to be for the people, not for the fulfillment of planning directives. Yet for the society at large, design remains an unclaimed possession," he says. He now works freelance, creating distinctive works on paper that mix art and design, and play with his favorite media: photography and silkscreening. Every year he produces original New Year's cards, which are sent to friends and colleagues. These rigorous black-and-white exercises stand apart from the kitschy cheerfulness normally associated with the genre. According to Berezovsky, graphic calligraphy of a silhouette, or proportion and balance of the abstract elements should bring purely visual pleasure to the card's recipient. The hand-made works have a meticulous quality, as if they came out of a printing press. His personal insignia "SKY" (the three

ИКСИД'75 ICSID'75
МОСКВА MOSCOW
КОНГРЕСС CONGRESS
ДИЗАЙН DESIGN
ДЛЯ ЧЕЛОВЕКА FOR MAN AND
И ОБЩЕСТВА SOCIETY
13. 10–16. 10. 1975

Der sowjetische Designer

Stuttgart

Ausstellung des All-Union-Instituts für technische Ästhetik der UdSSR
im Design Center Stuttgart des Landesgewerbeamts Baden-Württemberg
10.— 30. September 1976, Dienstag bis Sonntag 11—18 Uhr
Kienestraße 18, Eintritt frei

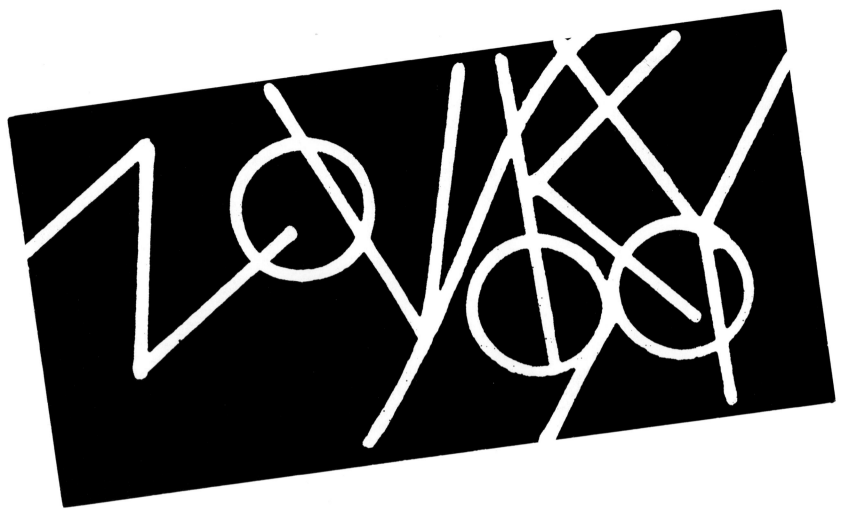

Above and opposite: New Year's cards, produced for friends, 1985–90.

last letters of his name) came about when he got tired of trying to Letraset his full signature onto one of these "mass" editions.

The political and artistic freedoms of the late 1980s led Berezovsky to undertake the theme of the political poster. This field gained a sudden popularity in the charged atmosphere of perestroika, yet most of the commercially successful posters produced then reminded Berezovsky of "enlarged caricatures." Images of Stalin taking aim at people with a rifle, or of the Kremlin surrounded by barbed wire, were not only historically false, he thought, they were in themselves like the cheap propaganda of the previous era. For his posters Berezovsky utilized documentary photographs, repeated and superimposed in his usual manner, to create an image of a crowd. Yet this crowd is very different from the one in his early work for ICSID: the darkening density, sinister colors, and instantly recognizable regalia of the Stalinist era, all

placed in an abstract context, create a lingering uneasiness and tension in these works.

Berezovsky lives in a dilapidated Constructivist building in the center of Moscow. The top floor, designed as an open roof garden, was built up and divided in the 1930s—in another blow to Constructivist avant-garde utopias. Berezovsky shares one of these unplanned apartments with his wife, a design critic, their daughter, and two small grandchildren; their apartment has long been known as a meeting place for the progressive artistic intelligentsia. In spite of the considerable respect that Berezovsky commands in his circles, a feeling of being "unclaimed" at times seems to overwhelm him. Yet he will proudly show a large silkscreen called *The Commandments of the Berezovsky Family*. A bold line of text at the top reads: "Do not make compromises." Perhaps this is why his work has always been on the sidelines of Russian design.

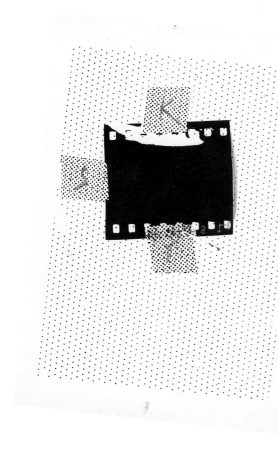

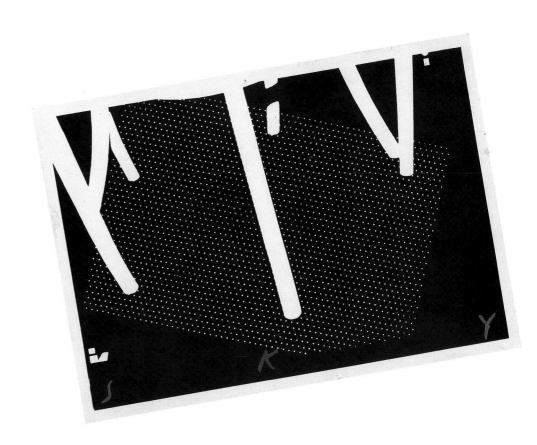

Above left: *Descent into Darkness*,
political poster, late 1980s.

Above: *The Year 1937*, political

ARZAMASOVA, EVZOVITCH, SVYATSKY [AES]

Literature has always occupied a special place in Russian culture, both in terms of official hierarchy and in the hearts of the people. Works of famous Russian writers and poets are studied in detail through all ten years of school. The antiquated practice of memorization that dates back to the nineteenth-century tradition of declamation and rhetorical eloquence is still practiced in Russian schools. Fragments of poetry and prose remain in the memory of every Soviet citizen as nationwide common narratives. Many writers and poets in Russia hold the status of cult figures, usually reserved in the West for pop singers and movie stars.

For these reasons, book design has for years been a prestigious and highly desirable field, one that has attracted creative individuals from various design professions. Yet the field was always filled with creative constraints, since classic literary works were considered an established canon open only to limited interpretations by art directors and illustrators. The team of Arzamasova, Evzovitch, and Svyatsky (AES) came to book design at the end of 1980s, when limitations regarding the treatment of once-sacred literary texts were finally lifted. Tania Arzamasova, born in 1955, and Lev Evzovitch, born in 1958, both graduated from the Moscow Architectural Institute. Arzamasova was a winner of several competitions, and one of her projects even got built during her school years—a war memorial in the institute's courtyard. The couple got married shortly after graduation. In 1987 they joined forces with Evgeny Svyatsky, who had studied book design at the Polygraphic Institute in Moscow. The multidisciplinary background of the group helped to formulate their broad-minded approach. The three designers entered the field with the goal of deconstructing the book, of turning it into a more complex, intense object by means of juxtaposing the text with elements borrowed from unlikely sources and genres.

The design of a classical Russian comedy, *Wit Works Woe,* written by Alexander Griboedov at the beginning of the nineteenth century, could serve as an example of the trio's method. The book consists of two volumes. The first contains the author's unabridged text, with illustrations from the original edition. The second, called "The Golden Notebook," contains only a strictly visual interpretation of the comedy's hidden complexities. *Wit Works Woe* tells the story of a young intellectual aristocrat upon return to his native Moscow after a self-imposed exile. Not only does he find his old love indifferent, but members of the city's high society, irritated by his biting irony, spread rumors about his insanity. The heartbroken hero is forced to leave the city again, this time forever. Various subplots of the story involving romance, political intrigue, and social satire are illustrated by the designers in a variety of graphic styles, from academic drawing to modernist collage to goofy comic strip. The two volumes together form "a difficult whole," to use the expression of Robert Venturi; they help reawaken this classic work of the past from the boredom of official recognition.

A Double Rainbow, designed by the AES trio, is said by its editor Marat Akchurin "to bridge Russian and American poetry." In his introduction to the book, which includes works by leading contemporary Russian and American poets, he asks, "If we speak in terms of human values, do our ideals really differ so drastically from those of the Americans?" The designers answer this question with a typically elegant design solution. A single large, multifaceted illustration, composed of many Soviet and American pop symbols, is featured in fragmentary form

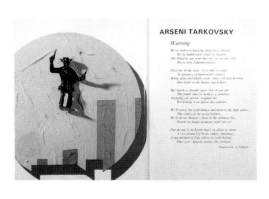

Top: Master illustration for the book
A Double Rainbow, 1988.

Above, left, center, and right:
A Double Rainbow, spreads and cover.

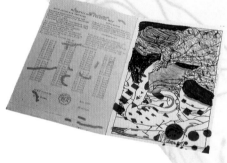

Above, top, center, and bottom:
Spreads from *Who Am I?*, book
project, 1989–90.

Right, top, center, and bottom:
Who Am I?, book project,
1989–90, illustrations based on
Nicola Poussin's *Apollo Inspiring an
Epic Poet*.

Above: *Who Am I?*, book project,
1989–90.

Wit Works Woe, book project, 1987–88. Left: Complete slipcovered set; center: volume with original text and illustrations; right: "The Golden Notebook."

throughout the text. The volume can be read in Russian from one side, in English from the other. Only in the middle of the book, where the two cultures meet, is the picture reproduced in its entirety. An unexpected juxtaposition of "serious" poetry with images of pop icons serves as a means of updating the text in the context of omnipresent mass culture.

Perhaps the most complex work by AES is a poetry volume called *Who Am I?,* which includes long poems of twenty-three contemporary Russian poets. Accordingly, the book appears to consist of twenty-three school notebooks, familiar to every Soviet youngster, all bound together. A painting by Poussin, *Apollo Inspiring an Epic Poet* from the Museum of Fine Arts in Moscow, appears on the cover as an outline, like a pattern from a children's coloring book. Progressively enlarged fragments of this image, colored by the designers, are scattered throughout the text, leading up to a detail of Apollo's index finger. His "dictating" gesture suggests a complex analogy with the art of poetry itself, which is constrained by its own archetypes and conventions. A military template, used by the designers as a coloring pattern, is enclosed in the volume as a bookmark. The various components of this design—classical painting, modern poetry, school notebooks, the "found

object" of the template—are tied together not only semantically, but visually, with their decorative ornamental quality. It is typical for the AES trio to combine conceptual rigor with the sensuous quality of their images.

A recent exhibition of work by AES was held in Germany and bore the title "The Pathetic Rhetoric." The designers take the sentimental, melodramatic narrative, so typical of the nineteenth-century realist tradition in Russia, and later revived by Socialist Realism, as the basis of their work. This source is then manipulated according to the methodologies of postmodernist artistic practice. The projects of Arzamasova, Evzovitch, and Svyatsky end up as a celebration of encyclopedic eclecticism, representative of the complexity and confusion of the current moment in the country's development.

Half-memorized passages from the masterpieces of Russian literature usually form the passive cultural baggage for the average reader. The books designed by Arzamasova, Evzovitch, and Svyatsky help to condition in the reader a critical outlook, to start a long-overdue reevaluation of familiar texts. The goal is a newly clarified perspective on the great authors that so shape the country's cultural life.

Wit Works Woe, book project, 1987–88, illustrations from "The Golden Notebook."

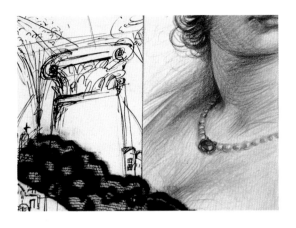

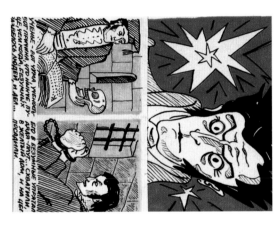

ALEXANDER BELOSLUDSEV

The style belonging to the Russian empire of the late nineteenth century is enjoying a popular revival. Attributes of that era's nascent bourgeois lifestyle—busy financial districts, glass-covered shopping promenades, fabled restaurants and entertainment—hold a particular appeal when compared to the grim reality that the country faces in the 1990s. By turning to early capitalist aesthetic ideals, the new Russia is attempting to shed seventy years of manipulative cultural domination of Communism. Historicism here means different things than in the Western postmodernist discourse; it stands for a moral position of purification, for desire of sophistication and quality. Yet the nineteenth-century aesthetic is not easy to grasp for contemporary designers. It is difficult to adopt the exuberant decorative language of that time in the very different historical conditions of modern Russia without retreating into kitsch. The work of calligrapher Alexander Belosludsev, however, seems to possess the unique sensibility of that bygone era.

Belosludsev was born in 1961. He studied at the Moscow Polygraphic Institute and graduated in 1984 hoping to work in calligraphy with new and existing handwritten type. This rare professional orientation is deeply rooted in his personality. Brought up in a village near Moscow, he was always drawn to the work of past masters. With his mild, restrained manners and his interest in the art, poetry, and music of an earlier era, he seems rather like a man of the past century. Not incidentally, Belosludsev's interests lie in the decorative, ornamental aspects of penmanship, rather than in conceptual design explorations. He wants to preserve and expand the disappearing cultural heritage of handwritten Cyrillic typeface.

In spite of the professional upsurge that Soviet calligraphy experienced in the 1970s and 1980s, the position of these artists, according to graphic design expert Maxim Zhukov, "held an uncertain place somewhere in between of popular hobbies and fine arts." Most likely, this would have been Belosludsev's place as well. The newly emerged historicist trend, favored by perestroika firms and businesses, suddenly has brought him numerous commissions for logos, stationery, and packaging. Belosludsev's graphics employ exotic motifs based on Old Russian calligraphy. Typically, a letter, handwritten in black ink, freely floats on a white background like a precious, unique artifact.

Belosludsev has experimented with various methods, using old brushes, goose quills, even twigs from a broom to create his work. Yet he is carried away by the sheer pleasure of "graphic needlework," not by a desire to break new ground in his field. He denies any conceptual interpretations of his work, but some of his designs for gift packaging and greeting cards seem to possess an intentional banality. Belosludsev, however, offers a different explanation: "Let's take the *Italian Capriccio* of Tchaikovsky, or his romances—they are really banal. But they were written by a true aristocrat of the spirit. He allowed himself to use a trite musical form in order to infuse it with certain personal qualities. My work is done in the same spirit."

Belosludsev distances himself from the methods of contemporary design, just as he has always disregarded the Soviet ideal of the collective good. He shows complete indifference to the concept of originality, as well as to that of irony; and he professes to be bored with new avant-garde movements. Yet the very application of his old-fashioned methods to the graphic products of new business enterprises provides a characteristic postmodernist "double coding." Archaic calligraphy takes on a different meaning on a

Above: Logo for XF, an export agency of the Art Foundation of Russia, 1988.

MOSCOW
palette

эффект

sheet of office stationery. At times, Belosludsev himself creates an approximation of a graphic collage. A logo for the perfume company Effect has a pair of hand-written *f*s which contrast with the other neatly typeset letters. A corporate identity program for the export firm Moscow Palette uses a varied graphic solution for each of the two words: a clean block for the first, and bold brush strokes for the second. These commercially successful projects map out a strong design direction already present in Belosludsev's work.

Still, Belosludsev thinks of himself as a calligrapher, not a designer. He participates in art shows, creates editions of prints, produces endless variations on old Cyrillic types. Is it not boring for him to write the same word over and over again, hundreds of times? Here he compares himself with a sportsman: "Is a swimmer bored with swimming for hours? In order to achieve something, one has to overcome mere excitement, mere physical pleasure." Against a background of general pessimism and uneasiness, Belosludsev's attitude appears to stand out as an example of the new purposefulness.

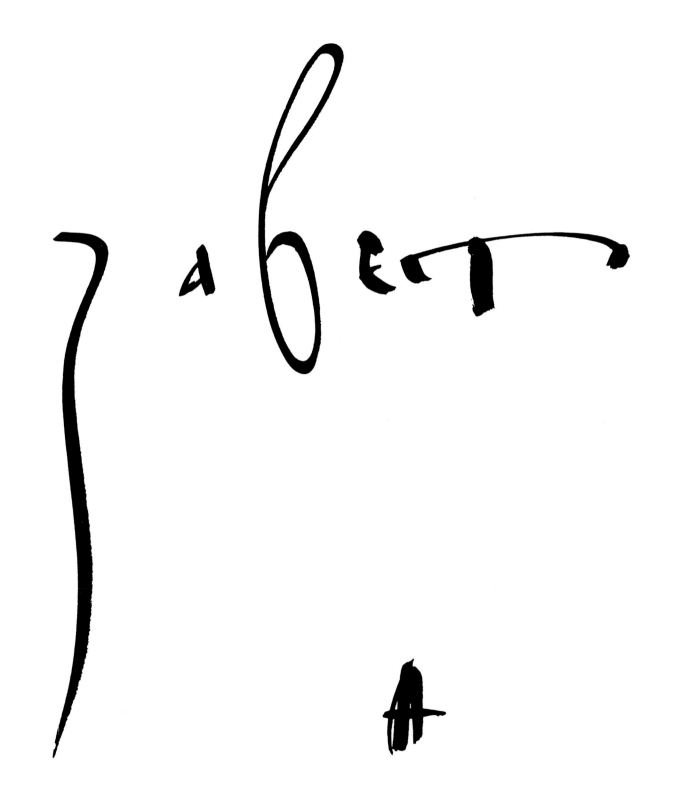

print

entre

Above: Gift packaging designs, 1989.

Above left: Logo for Print, a Soviet-British publishing agency.

Left: Logo for Entre, a Soviet-French joint venture.

Opposite: Designs for holiday greeting cards, "Happy Birthday" (top) and "Congratulations" (bottom).

ANDREY SECHIN

According to a popular Russian story, the King of Sweden once sent an intricate present to the Russian Czar. This amazing gift— a life-size, mechanical wind-up flea—was promptly forwarded to the Czar's armories in Tula with an order to produce another technically superior gadget that would put the Swedes to shame. After some weeks, the armories returned the flea to the king; it appeared the artisans could do nothing to improve upon it. Yet when Swedish experts examined it under a microscope, they noticed almost invisible shoes at the end of each of the flea's legs. In their antiquated armories, the Russians did the impossible—they shoed the Swedish flea—and the Czar was ecstatic.

Even though the legend has a prerevolutionary origin, it was extensively promoted by Soviet propaganda during the years of the Cold War. The myth of the Russian genius, capable of single-handedly beating technologically advanced Western competition, helped to cultivate the national pride. Many Soviet scientific and cultural endeavors were set up and generously financed by the government to furnish further proof of Russian superiority. An entire generation of people grew up with the belief that Khruschev's challenge—"to leave America behind"—would be met in a matter of only a few years. Glasnost publicly exposed the meaninglessness of this propaganda race, conducted at the expense of the Russian people, who themselves were deprived of basic conveniences in their living and working conditions.

Much like the legendary Russian craftsmen, Andrey Sechin faces an impossible professional challenge. He

is a designer of packaging for food and beverage products in a country infamous for its material shortages. Sechin's products are commissioned by a state agency for exportation abroad, in exchange for much needed hard currency. Thus, his packaging becomes crucial to those few Russian foods and wines that are chosen to compete on the free Western market. Export companies usually create new labels for such merchandise, and Sechin has become an expert in this task. He knows how to dress Russian products in such a way that they can seduce the discriminating Western consumer.

Sechin has created an impressive portfolio of printed material, working from his small apartment far from the fashionable city center. His bathroom doubles as a self-made laboratory, where he has invented and perfected a way of making photostats with a standard photo enlarger. "One has to be an engineer, a chemist, and a physicist to do packaging here," he explains. He makes Letraset by hand and uses hand-colored swatches to imitate a Pantone color selector.

Sechin has been attracted to package design for a long time. Born in 1960, he used to collect labels from wine bottles as a child. Bright foreign labels formed the prized core of his collection. Early on he tried to create his own labels, drawing them by hand with colored pencils. After graduating from the 1905 Art School he chose to work for a state agency responsible for food packaging. His breakthrough came in 1986. A Spanish company that wanted to distribute Russian sparkling wines in Europe chose a bottle with a Sechin-designed label. When the Spaniards were politely directed toward better wines available in the same collection, their response was, "We don't care about the wine—they are all bad—but we certainly want the label."

After that Sechin began to work almost exclusively on export production. This not only assures him

Right: Label design, Elegia (Elegy)
chocolate bar.

Above: Logo, Rot Front chocolate factory.

superior quality printing and execution, but allows him to appeal to the Western customer with work that exudes a spirit of Russian exoticism. Thus his labels for Saint-Petersburg wine spell out the title in elaborate Cyrillic letters, without translation, thus projecting a distinctly Russian aura. The design is formally restrained and contemporary, yet it retains the preciousness of an historical artifact. Sechin's aesthetic ideal lies neither in Old Russian nor in Constructivist culture. He finds inspiration in Peter Carl Fabergé, the celebrated jeweler, French by origin, who was working in Russia at the turn of the century. Fabergé imperial eggs—jewelled gifts presented on Easter to members of the Czar's family—became a timeless symbol of material and artistic perfection.

In the late 1980s, Western consumers saw a lot of what designer and critic Steven Heller called "retro packaging." This type of packaging retained a traditional, nostalgic flavor, emphasizing a long-gone, sometimes fictitious history of the product as a proven sign of quality. Inside Russia, the epithet "prerevolutionary," once derogatory, came to signify value, taste, and sophistication. Sechin intuitively felt attracted to design inspired by the past. His personal approach became a marketing strategy for his clients, who regarded his work as an exotic Russian variant of "retro packaging."

Not all of his designs are immediate hits. Some clients have found his images to be too refined to make an impact on the supermarket shelf. For instance, a faint daguerreotype image of Red Square, which Sechin used for the label of Zhigul beer when it was exported to England, had to be replaced with a catchy color photograph when an American distributor brought the same beer to California. And his chocolate packaging for the Moscow state confectionery has been criticized as elitist. According to Sechin, chocolate, as a luxury item on the Russian table, should evoke "a special, romantic feeling." Its

packaging is correspondingly elegant and abstract. Even in these works, printed at the local typographies for internal consumption, Sechin manages to maintain the highest possible quality of printing.

The legendary artisans who shoed the Swedish flea were generously rewarded by the Czar. For Sechin the award came from abroad. In 1991 he was invited by a Chicago-based firm, Source, Inc., to take up a six-month working stint in America. The invitation allows Sechin to compare his work with that which is being made in the West. Only then can the true measure of his ingenuity be taken.

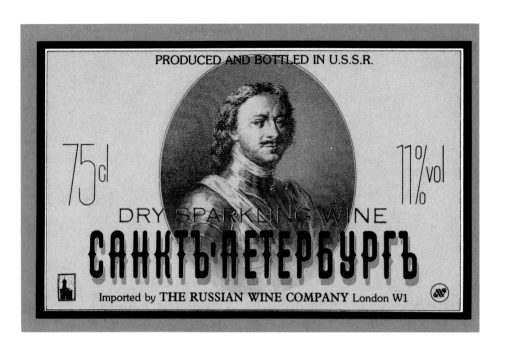

Above: Label design, "Saint-Petersburg" sparkling wine.

Left: Label design, "Saint-Petersburg" red wine.

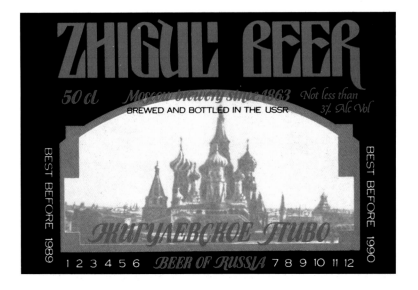

Above: Label design, Vechernii Arbat (Evening Arbat Street) non-alcoholic carbonated beverage.

Left, top: Label design, Zhigul beer, as distributed in the United States.

Left, bottom: Label design, Zhigul beer, as distributed in Great Britain.

Opposite, top: Label design, Tshelkunchik (The Nutcracker) chocolate bar.

Opposite, bottom: Label design, Zhiguli (Zhiguli River) chocolate bar.

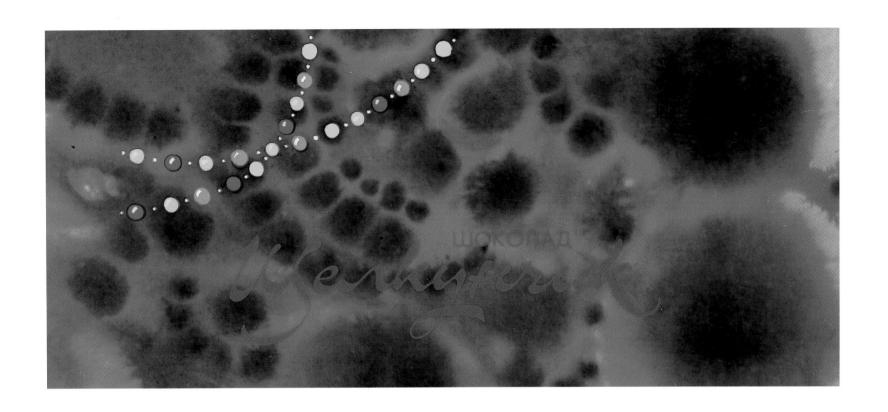

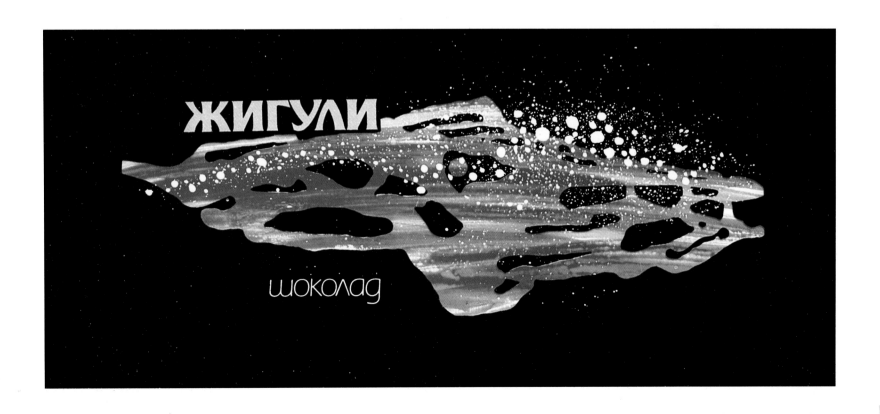

HELENA KITAYEVA

The republic of Belorussia (now Belarus) was known primarily for its farming, milk and meat production, and political conservatism. Almost completely destroyed during World War II by the Nazis, its cities and factories were subsequently rebuilt; the cultural life in the republic, however, never reached any level of sophistication. An insipid, provincial version of Socialist Realism firmly established itself in art, architecture, and design. Memories of alternative artistic expression were routinely repressed; undesirable artworks of the past were locked up in museum storage.

After several decades of such a cultural vacuum, few could remember that in the 1920s, Belorussia boasted an art institution that could be compared to the Bauhaus in terms of importance. The School of Unovis was established in the small town of Vitebsk, in the northwest of the republic. The town, with its narrow hilly streets and colorful Jewish neighborhood, was immortalized in the early paintings of Marc Chagall; the artist was born there and went on to head the local art school. In 1919 Kazimir Malevich succeeded Chagall and he created Unovis (school of Affirmers of the New Art), where the major principles of Suprematism were formulated.

In the mid-1980s, as the ban on nonfigurative painting was slowly lifted, young art and design students in Belorussia began to reclaim the work of "the Vitebsk Renaissance" as their unique cultural heritage. Helena Kitayeva first visited Vitebsk in 1988, two years after her graduation from the Belorussian State Institute of Fine Arts. She had been commissioned to create environmental graphics and posters for a festival of contemporary song. As Kitayeva walked through the streets of Vitebsk, the legacy of Unovis exerted a profound influence on her.

She thought of her mother, a textile printer, and of the geometric patterns she played with at her home. She remembered how she had failed art classes at school, because her drawings were "constructed, not drawn from life." Convinced that "Constructivism runs in her blood," Kitayeva found it possible to adopt the style of the 1920s as her own working method. She believed that her cultural mission was to restore a missing link in Russian culture, by bringing the artistic language of the Constructivist avant-garde back into mainstream design.

How valid is this approach? The Constructivists themselves would have argued that the language of design should be of its own time, that it may not borrow from previous historical periods. For almost a century, the concept of original work has remained a cornerstone of the avant-garde theory. Yet in the early 1980s an increasing number of young Western artists attempted a critique of originality by appropriating existing avant-garde languages and visual images for their own work. Kitayeva's design could be placed in this postmodernist framework as well. By focusing exclusively on the decorative aspects of Constructivism, devoid of their former semantic and political significance, Kitayeva creates a simulation of Constructivism, as visually engaging as her historical precedent.

In a poster for a tour of the Soviet Union by the English National Opera, Kitayeva borrowed the drawing of a human figure from Malevich, which was skillfully positioned to represent the typically Russian image of a herald, with arms spread in a universal sign of exclamation. Using red, white, and

Right: *Opera on the Russian Stage*, poster for the English National Opera's tour in the Soviet Union, 1990.

Left: *The First Soviet Car*, part of
The First Soviets poster series,
Belarus Publishers, Minsk, 1990.

black—the trademark colors of Constructivist graphics—she immediately identified the cultural and geographic background of the advertised event.

When Russian art started to enjoy popularity and collectors' attention abroad, commercial applications of Kitayeva's talent became obvious to many entrepreneurs. Thus, Belarus Publishers engaged Kitayeva to create a series of limited-edition posters, devoted to innovative Soviet means of transportation, from a truck of 1924 to the first Earth satellite of 1957. The title of the collection—*The First Soviet*—harks back to the Cold War propaganda concerning the superiority of socialism, while a red background covered with state regalia seems to capitalize on newly fashionable Soviet imagery. The overall polished graphic design of the series has the flavor more of Art Deco than of Constructivism. For Kitayeva this was not a casual choice. She wants to investigate the various alternative routes of the Russian avant-garde that might have existed had the movement not been suppressed so forcefully in the 1930s. Not incidentally, she chose Art Deco—the most commercial, stylistically refined application of Western Modernist ideals—for *The First Soviet* poster series.

Kitayeva treated another project for Belarus Publishers in a very different way. A children's book called *The Suprematic ABC* aims at introducing the Constructivist idiom to young readers. The book features celebrated icons of the Russian avant-garde with their corresponding first letter. On some pages Kitayeva includes her own designs for Suprematism-inspired small domestic objects: scissors, a key, an alarm clock. Thanks to a creative, energetic layout and to the use of specially designed Suprematic type, the patchwork of images is organized into a unified book-object. For a young reader, still surrounded by Socialist Realism-style books, the *Suprematic ABC* becomes an embodiment of Constructivism itself, perhaps the reader's only experience of this alternative visual system.

The complex cultural situation of the early Russian avant-garde—extremely popular abroad and not completely accepted in its own homeland—conditions the perception of Kitayeva's work. Amidst depression and indifference, her images may strike some as too forceful and blindly optimistic, yet they might be just fitting for the would-be Constructivists of the next generation.

Above left: *The First Soviet Locomotive*, part of *The First Soviets* poster series, Belarus Publishers, Minsk, 1990.

Above: *The First Soviet Sputnik.*

Left: *The First Soviet Freight Engine.*

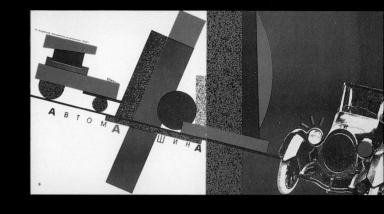

The Suprematic ABC, children's
book, Belarus Publishers, Minsk,
1990. Above: The alphabet.; above
right: letter A (automobile by Ivan
Kudryashov); right: letter K
(construction by Liubov Popova).

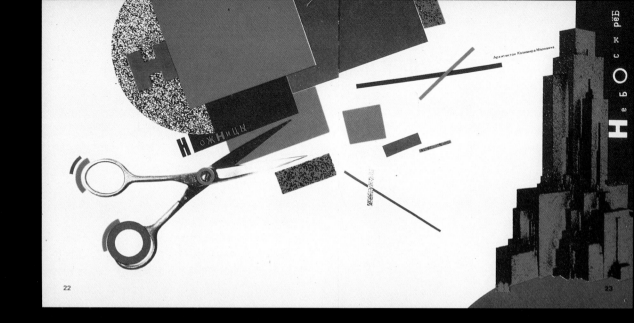

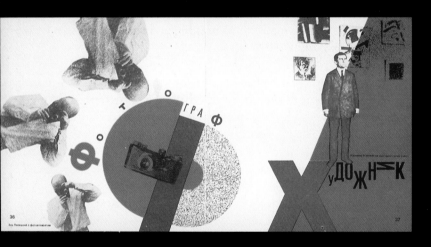

The Suprematic ABC children's book, Belarus Publishers, Minsk, 1990. Top: *Letter N* (skyscraper by Kazimir Malevich); above: *letter Ph* (portrait of photographer El Lissitzky) and *letter Kh* (portrait of artist Kazimir Malevich); right: *letter U* (detail of a poster by Alexander Lavinsky).

Poster Design

Opposite: Poster for *Nostalgia*, a
film by Andrei Tarkovsky, 1988.

IGOR MAISTROVSKY

One of the few creative fields in Russia that experienced a creative surge during the 1970s was that of theater and film poster design. A powerful influence on Soviet poster artists came from Poland, a country that by the 1960s had assumed a leading position in the field of poster design. The school of Polish poster design was born after World War II, in a cultural landscape of complete desolation. A surrealist orientation and sense of the macabre characterized the posters; hand-drawn images and type, reproduced by lithography, were the favored design techniques. Polish artists distrusted the prevailing realistic mode, favoring instead the use of visual metaphor. The international Warsaw Biennial, established in 1966, brought the achievements of the Polish poster to the world at large. Nowhere did its influence prove as strong as in the Soviet Union. For Soviet designers, Poland was the West, and its Biennial the only accessible peephole into a foreign culture. Surrealist imagery appeared exciting and subversive compared to the vapid formulas of Socialist Realism. And the level of sophistication of the visual metaphors in the Polish work clearly exceeded that of average Soviet graphics.

Igor Maistrovsky first realized this as a student at the Stroganoff Art School in Moscow. Although he had specialized in industrial design, after his graduation in 1973 he decided to concentrate on poster graphics. Eventually, he found a few long-term clients: Gostsyrk, the managing body of the State Soviet Circus, and Reclamfilm, the state agency of film advertising. Steadily producing twenty to thirty posters a year, he has become one of the leading poster designers in the country, working alone in a small studio in a communal apartment.

After many years of fascination with the metaphorical approach of Polish design, he is no longer sure of its creative potential. "A metaphor leads to banality, once its meaning is captured and digested," he explains. Maistrovsky works on a more personal level, creating a synthetic image that often incorporates his own artistic process into the poster's contents. He uses pastels, colored pencils, and textured paper throughout his oeuvre; rarely does one find a typeset line in his work.

Maistrovsky's poster for the film *Nostalgia* is representative. Made by the late Russian director Andrei Tarkovsky during a long sojourn in Italy, this largely autobiographical film reflects on the mental state of a Russian poet who lives away from his homeland. Maistrovsky's own symbols of Italy and Russia—the Tower of Pisa, snowflakes, white birch trees—together form an image of a burning votive candle. The poster for *The Sacrifice,* the last film by Tarkovsky, goes well beyond obvious metaphor, never allowing for a single interpretation. In the disquieting poster, the habitual signs of domestic security are seen as fractured and split, and the fate of civilization appears in jeopardy. Maistrovsky shows a paper-thin tablecloth hovering in the nothingness of a black background; the latter has been a favorite expressive device of his for years. It is present, for example, in a poster for *The Feast of Valthasar,* a grotesque comedy about the infamous night feasts that Stalin regularly held with a group of his closest henchmen (some of whom were never seen alive after these "celebrations"). A bare fish skeleton bearing the profiles of several easily recognized political figures reflects the film's comic and ghastly absurdity.

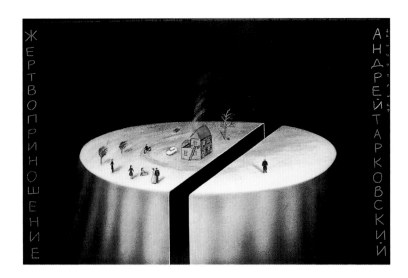

Top: Poster for *The Sacrifice*, a film by Andrei Tarkovsky, 1988.

Above: Poster for *One Flew Over The Cuckoo's Nest*, a film by Milos Forman, 1988.

When Maistrovsky worked on the poster for *One Flew Over The Cuckoo's Nest*, he wanted to bring the film closer to the perception of his fellow Russians. He felt the acute relevance of the story to his country's experience: that of the labor camps and psychiatric clinics used to confine political dissidents. Thus, the poster features some elements that do not appear in the movie—a long barracks, the identical silhouettes of prisoners—which hold a special significance for the Russian audience. This work is, perhaps, Maistrovsky's closest approximation of a political poster. He does not feel attracted to, nor does he believe in, any one political affiliation.

In his series of advertising posters for the State Circus, started in the mid-1980s, each poster had to be devoted to a particular performer. Following this convention, Maistrovsky nevertheless attempts to express the spirit of the circus in general, to transmit its magic energy, full of humor and danger. He carefully studied Lubok, a form of Old Russian folk art, while working on the series. Lubok pictures were lithographed on paper, hand-colored, and sold at the bazaars for display in peasants' homes. Maistrovsky found the festive carnival imagery fitting for his circus theme, and has used it to a striking effect.

The changes of glasnost have opened up many previously forbidden creative themes. Ironically, as many new kinds of entertainment became available, public interest in the cinema has plummeted, and so has demand for Maistrovsky's posters. "There are no creative limits now. An artist can say anything," Maistrovsky explains. "Alas, unconditional freedom always begets satiety."

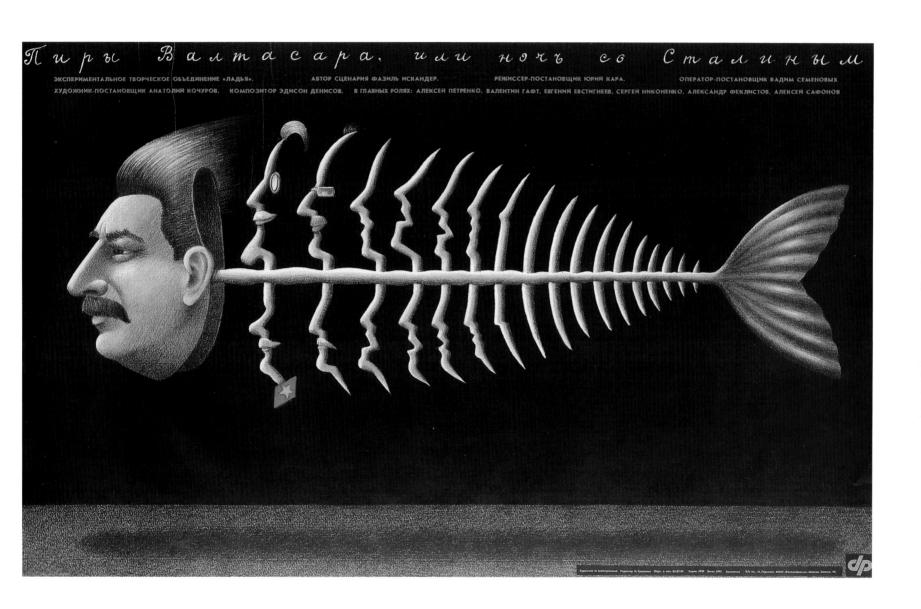

Above: Poster the film *The Feast of Valthasar*, 1990.

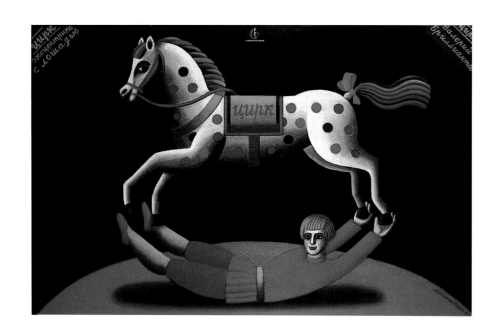

Right, top and bottom: Circus
posters, 1986.

Opposite: Poster for the film *The
Cold Summer of the Year 1953*,
1988.

ANDREY KOLOSOV AND VALERIA KOVRIGINA

In 1988 Sotheby's held an unprecedented auction in Moscow. For the first time, the works of living Russian artists were offered for sale to the Western art market, occasionally attracting six-digit bids and making artists rich overnight. The sensational success of this enterprise not only made Russian art a valuable and fashionable commodity, it also profoundly affected the country's future cultural development. Some artists, who since the 1960s have found a safe haven in the field of graphic design, have now returned to painting, offering their work to an ever-increasing number of collectors.

Husband-and-wife team Andrey Kolosov and Valeria Kovrigina straddle the worlds of art and graphic design. They first gained notoriety in the late 1980s with their sinister, noncommissioned political posters, manually silkscreened by the couple. Their studio is located in a Moscow building that Stalin gave as a present to the actors of his favorite Moscow Art Theater in 1938, amid the terror of political purges. It is ironic that Kolosov and Kovrigina have set up their studio there, in an attic equipped with a stationary camera, silkscreening equipment, and self-made flat files. Technical difficulties usually limit their palette to gray, black, and red, but the vigor of their creative energy knows few limitations.

Born in 1955, Andrey Kolosov never had any professional schooling. Instead, he and his future wife studied rock music and participated in the Russian hippie scene. They started their graphic design career in 1975, with the first commissions coming, not surprisingly, from the music industry. Their fascination with Western art and photography,

particularly the influence of Andy Warhol and Gilbert & George, is evident in the designers' early work. A cover for the final record by Alexandr Tsfasman, for example, features a Warhol-like composition made with the pianist's image. The fact that this is Tsfasman's last recording is expressed as by the musician's face gradually going out of focus.

Kolosov and Kovrigina continue to use photography as the basis of their work. The designers had personal reasons to start a series of political posters in 1989: sixteen members of Kovrigina's family were imprisoned or executed during Stalin's reign. These politically charged works not only allowed for the expression of their inner feelings and beliefs, it also provided the couple with a small flow of Western art buyers. Exhibited at a Moscow art show, many of these posters created a scandal even in the liberated climate of perestroika. A sheet entitled *Happy Holidays Comrades!* managed to irritate viewers from virtually every layer of Russian society. Hardliners objected to the comparing of Stalin's atrocities to Lenin's memory, reformers protested the profanation of the image of Madonna and Child, aesthetes opposed the mockery of a Leonardo painting from the Hermitage.

Kolosov and Kovrigina's method—a postmodernist collage of dissimilar elements, selected as signs from a vast library of the world's cultures—retains an uncommon emotional appeal. While the concepts behind posters like *Homo Soveticus* or *Beat the Whites*

Left, top: Theater poster for the play *Soviet Poetry of the 1930–1940s*, Theater-Studio of Moscow University, 1989.

Left, bottom: Theater poster for the play *The Dark Man*, Theater-Studio of Moscow University, 1988.

with The Red Wedge may appear trivial, the works nevertheless hold as powerful visual statements. In fact, their technical language, severely limited by the designers' self-made technological base, serves them well, providing a distinctive and consistent look. The designers bring the same qualities to a few commissioned works, such as their posters for the Theater-Studio of Moscow University. *The Dark Man,* a black comedy about the life of Stalin, is represented by a broken plaster mask of the dictator, covered with absurdist footnotes. The air of the carnival is strongly present in this and other Kolosov and Kovrigina works. According to a seminal study by Mikhail Bakhtin, the carnival, with its nonsense, obsenity, and laughter, expresses people's essential longing for freedom. "Postmodernism needs the carnival," wrote Peter Wollen, discussing the work of Russian artists Komar and Melamid, the founders of Sots Art. The practice of Sots Art, which since the 1970s has called for the creative appropriation and subversion of Soviet official imagery, still exerts a profound influence over Kolosov and Kovrigina's graphics.

The precious balance between farce and tragedy, so typical of the Russian people's life, inevitably finds reflection in the designers oeuvre. A series of AIDS posters, created in 1990, exposes a darker side to their imagination. Mirror-reflected photographic compositions, frightening in their supernatural symmetry, evoke an apocalyptic menace. Such a satanic, mystical vision of the disease reflects the view of the Russian society at large, which has not yet come to grips with the gruesome reality of the epidemic.

Andrey Kolosov has few illusions about the social necessity of his work. "Ultimately, it is our personal artistic ego that motivates everything we do," he says. "I hope to be able to hire a printer, to set up a small printing press in this studio. Russian poster art is on the decline. We hope to revive it here."

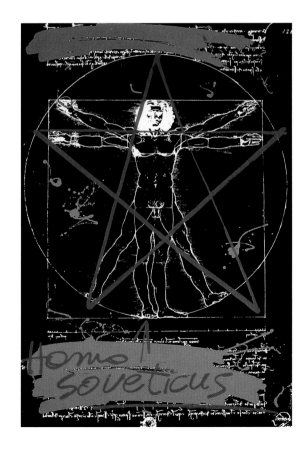

Above: *Beat the Whites with the Red Wedge*, political poster, 1990.

Right, top: *Requiem*, political poster, 1990.

Right, bottom: *Homo Soveticus*, political poster, 1990.

Above and opposite: Posters on
the subject of AIDS, 1990.

YURI BOKSER

"Of all the arts, our most important one is cinema." This Lenin quote used to decorate one wall in virtually every Russian movie theater. Properly understood as an essential mass medium since the early years of the Bolshevik Revolution, cinema has been a powerful, yet subtle, instrument of propaganda. In the absence of newspaper and television advertising, the movie poster has evolved as a nearly exclusive way of gaining public attention and providing necessary visual information. Reclamfilm, the state agency of movie advertising, boasted its own printing presses, where poster editions of half a million copies were not unusual.

It was at this agency that poster designer Yuri Bokser got his start. Born in 1953, Bokser studied at the Moscow Architectural Institute and went through three obligatory years of internship at an architectural office after his graduation. Leaving architecture behind in 1980, he began his ten-year stint in poster design under the aegis of Reclamfilm. His new career brought him a handful of international awards and firmly established his position in the graphic arts. In the design of his posters, Bokser always favors work with a strong conceptual basis. In a graphic project for the Society of Landmark Preservation, he uses an academically drawn figure of Atlas whose lower half is missing. Hanging in a void, the statue supports an architrave with the inscription, "There is no future without the past." In this early poster, the rationalism of concept and execution betrays the work of a one-time architect.

In search for a more flexible design language, Bokser started to use manipulated photographic images.

Photomontage was first popularized in the late 1920s by Alexander Rodchenko, who sought to incorporate figurative imagery into the framework of Constructivist aesthetics. Bokser is more interested in semantic transformations than in formal exercises. For a poster announcing the documentary film *I Do Not Like,* devoted to the memory of celebrated Russian bard Vladimir Vysotsky, Bokser used a kitschy postcard image torn into pieces covered with traces of lipstick. The poster reflects on the disintegration of this artist's true personality through an overzealous cult following.

Bokser took a more lighthearted approach in a double poster for the 1970s French classic *A Man and a Woman* and its insipid sequel, *A Man and a Woman: Twenty Years Later.* One half has a straightforward blow-up of a well-known stock photograph from the movie. In the other half, Bokser reused the same format, mockingly adding the signs of the aging actors' decay: wrinkles, unkempt beard, ragged skin. "This design would probably get censored in France, but here in Russia it has been posted all over," he jokes. His biting irony has also found expression in a series of political posters created in the liberated atmosphere of glasnost. One of them shows Lenin's face wrinkled in an unusual grimace of remorse. Its title—"The most human of all humans," a hyperbolic description of Lenin by the poet Mayakovsky—has become one of those ubiquitous slogans stuck in the memory of every Russian citizen. Through the subject's changed facial expression, Bokser offers a literal and visually shocking interpretation of the slogan. The other poster—an enlarged copy of a commercial calendar featuring Gorbachev's official portrait (his birthmark was routinely airbrushed out until 1987)—elaborates on the kitsch dimension in representative portraits of Soviet leaders.

In these works, Bokser is indebted to the theory and practice of the Sots Art movement, conceived in

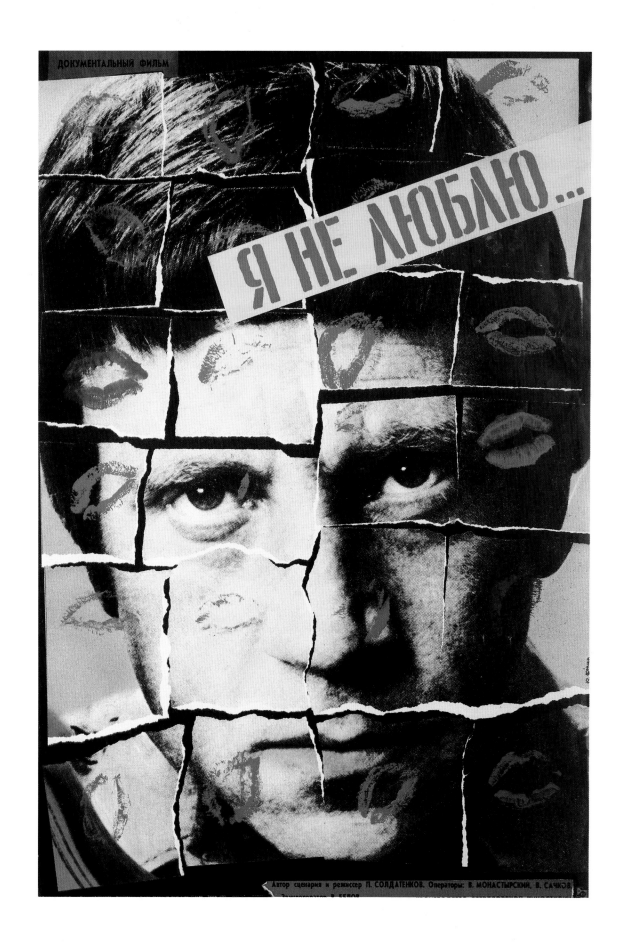

Right: Poster for the film *I Do Not Like*, 1989.

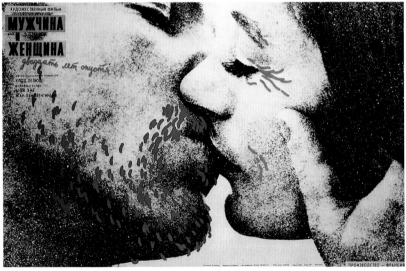

Above, top and bottom: Double poster for the films *A Man and a Woman* and *A Man and a Woman: 20 Years Later*, 1988.

Moscow in 1972 by a duo of dissident artists, Komar and Melamid. The artists, who later emigrated to the West, first began to appropriate official imagery of Socialist Realism and Soviet mass media, transforming them into a contemporary language of their own subversive art. According to Margarita Tupitsyn's analysis in the book *Margins of Soviet Art,* the task of Sots Art, "to dismantle the system of sacred referents of totalitarian culture without abandoning its generic features and mythical language, constituted an unprecedented example of postmodernist praxis." In the West, Sots Art has long been acknowledged among the major achievements in contemporary art.

The Russian public is still ambivalent about such deconstruction of the country's cultural stereotypes. Bokser's Lenin poster became a center of controversy at a Moscow exhibition in 1990; people covered its margins with their hand-written remarks. "Get out of Russia!" wrote one observer, adding a few anti-Semitic insults; "The best work of the show," countered another visitor.

Bokser made a brilliant use of altered photography in his award-winning poster for the film *Stalin's Funeral.* Using a famous archival photo of Stalin on his deathbed, the designer skillfully "opened" one of the deceased dictator's eyes. The uncanny realism of the image provided a strong visual metaphor for the movie, which is concerned with the spirit of Stalinism still alive in the depths of Russian society.

Bokser spent most of the year 1991 abroad. Was it his growing international recognition, or the threat of the "Get out of Russia!" scribbles that prompted him to look for work in the West? Bokser explains that he lost interest in making film posters, as the Russian movie industry has largely dried up. The signs bearing Lenin's words on the supremacy of cinema have already disappeared in Russia, sharing their fate with other traces of the old Communist propaganda.

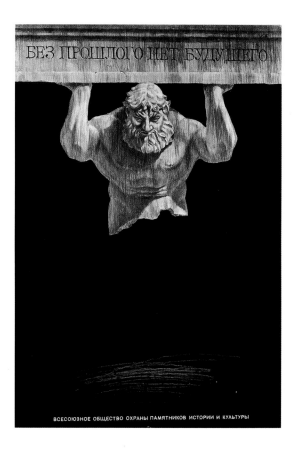

Above: *There Is No Future Without The Past*, poster for the Society of Landmarks Preservation.

Left: Poster for the film *Tower*, 1988.

„Самый человечный человек".

Above: Poster for the film *Stalin's Funeral*, 1991, Grand Prix at the World Festival in Chaumont, France.

Right: *Gorbachev*, political poster, 1990.

Opposite: *The Most Human of All Humans*, political poster, 1990. The top-right corner of the poster is covered with handwritten public responses.

Design for the Future

VLAD KIRPICHEV AND SCHOOL-STUDIO EDAS

"The sensation that the 'tomorrow' of Russian architecture has all the reasons to be even more dismal that 'today' has come to the profession only recently," says Moscow architect Andrey Bokov. "It becomes increasingly clear that concern for the future is not seen in designing visionary cities, it is in our care for the professional schools."

Even though the architectural schools in Russia preserve the memories of their once-glorious traditions, they do not have much to offer to the students of the 1990s. Critics agree that their ossified methodology, developed in accordance with a rigid hierarchical educational system, is in need of a complete overhaul. In this climate, alternative schools are especially important, providing a valuable precedent for a new system of architectural education.

School-Studio EDAS (Experimental Children's Architectural Studio) is at the forefront of experimental education in Russia. Its goal is to introduce children to architecture early: students range in age from six to sixteen years old. The founder of EDAS, Vlad Kirpichev, graduated from the Moscow Architectural Institute in 1975. One of the most brilliant students of his generation, he won a number of architectural competitions as a student, including the prestigious UNESCO prize contest of 1972. In 1977, while going through his obligatory years of internship, he assembled five schoolchildren from the neighborhood and told them about architecture. Soon, informal classes in drawing and composition developed. "Perhaps, it was children who helped their teacher to turn his bitterness of professional disappointment into a positive creative program," says Andrey Rodionov, Kirpichev's long-time teaching colleague. When EDAS made its first public presentation of work, the compositional complexity and technical precision of the drawings startled observers. Inevitably, the question of fraud came up: was it the teacher who did all the work, rather than his pupils?

As the methodology of EDAS was opened up for scrutiny, it soon became obvious that it was the children's collective creativity that had accounted for such superior work. The key to the school's success has been in its comprehensive approach to education. In addition to architecture, children study literature and nature; they listen to classical music and provide visual interpretations; they attend theater and film screenings and try their hands at stage design. Above all, it is play that serves as an organizing principle for the school. Play is incorporated not only into recreation, but into work and study as well.

Why is it necessary to start this complex process with six-year-olds? At this age "children are filled with a bright hope, which eventually gets lost later," explains educator Boris Barkhin. "Cognition of the world paralyzes the child's ability of an adequate artistic reflection. The constant images are being fixed in the child's imagination, like for example, a profile contour of a horse. One can ask him to draw a horse, and it is always going to be a profile." Kirpichev fights such stereotypes through a structuralist approach in his art class. When his pupils are asked to draw a leaf, for instance, they are advised that there is

равновесие

конструкция

пересечение

наложение

структура

симметрия

ассимметрия

дерево

сложное

простое

разрушение.

Left: Max Baryshnikov (16 years old)/ School-Studio EDAS, *Transformations*, 1988.

Above: Sasha Lezhava (15 years old)/School-Studio EDAS, *The Tower of Babel*, 1988.

Right, top: Tania Kirs (10 years old)/School-Studio EDAS, *The Doll*, 1989.

Right, bottom: Vlad Tulupov (14 years old)/School-Studio EDAS, *Horizontal-Vertical Skyscraper*, 1988.

more in it that meets the eye, namely a structure of a shaft and veins. "The task is to transform their imitative mode of work into a constructive one," says Kirpichev. Works in different media are produced, according to the rules of architectural form. Kirpichev considers architecture a universal craft. He observes, "A serious, deep study of this one craft influences the development of a child's intellect and aesthetics much more than a superficial general knowledge of all the arts."

To master the craft of architecture, the children enrolled at EDAS have to ascend the three levels of the school's educational system. The first is a preparatory cycle, to guide pupils into the spirit of the studio. It serves as a kind of creative quarantine, and helps to remove children's occasional fear of self-expression. The main level has a core study program that covers diverse project activities. The school takes a universalist approach, stressing the futility of academic divisions. Finally, there is the third level, the aim of which is the making of a complete artistic object. Diverse and unusual assignments, such as "Letters of the Alphabet," "Skyscraper," and "Architectural Cake," have served as projects during the School-Studio's history.

The Renaissance-derived system of maestro and pupils is clearly evident during this last stage of school. Here, Kirpichev sees himself as "a communicator between the children and architecture." His critics prefer to call him a dictator who dominates that precarious, volatile relationship. "One feels the pressure of the instructor's powerful, dictating hand," stated one entry in the comment book of EDAS exhibition. Kirpichev believes that a certain domination over his students is only natural. "It would be strange if a teacher did not influence his pupils through his attitudes, preferences, and convictions. Studying, after all, means stylization. One

becomes a master only when one attains a peculiar, personal vision."

Not all of the graduates of School-Studio EDAS continue their careers in architecture or design. While at the school they are certain to get a powerful creative charge, their exposure to the real world of Russian design can be more painful. "I would like to join a monastery . . . with my teacher and studio friends," reads the statement of one of the EDAS young students, as if anticipating the difficulty of pursuing a real-life design career. Kirpichev is fully aware of this. He is attempting to reorganize EDAS so that students can continue at the school beyond age sixteen, at the college level. He has established an architectural studio to work on actual commissions with his brightest students. After many years of voluntary withdrawal from the practice of architecture, his desire to build is understandable. Kirpichev's projects so far—playgrounds, verandas, and summer houses—have the playful quality of children's work; apparently, the influence between teacher and students goes both ways. A continuity between the school projects and real architectural work deserves attention, as it delineates at least one possible future for the young Russian designers.

Above: Alan Dzodziev (8 years old)/School-Studio EDAS, *Leaning Skyscraper,* 1989.

Above right: School-Studio EDAS, *Letters E, D, A,* and *C* (EDAS), group exercise, 1988.

Opposite: Max Baryshnikov (16 years old)/School-Studio EDAS, *Letter W,* 1988.

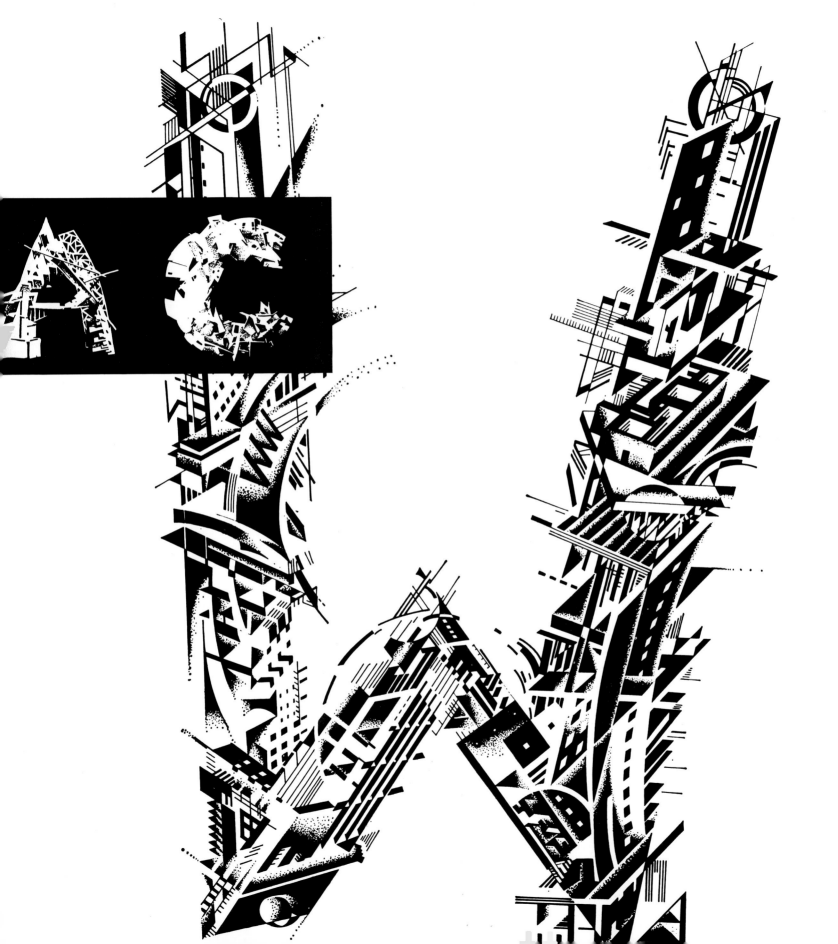

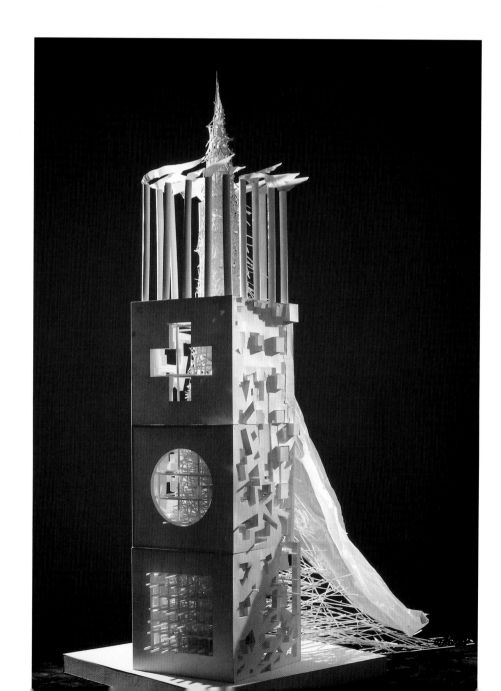

Top: Vlad Kirpichev, *Garden bench*, 1986, project (in collaboration with Liudmila Kirpicheva and Max Baryshnikov).

Right: Vlad Kirpichev, *Moscow Architecton*, Christmas-cake design for Steelcase Design Partnership, New York, 1989 (in collaboration with Liudmila Kirpicheva and Max Baryshnikov).

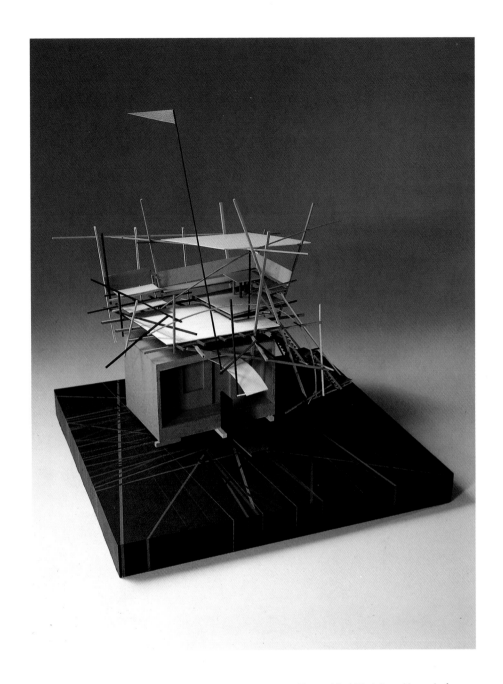

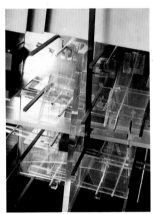

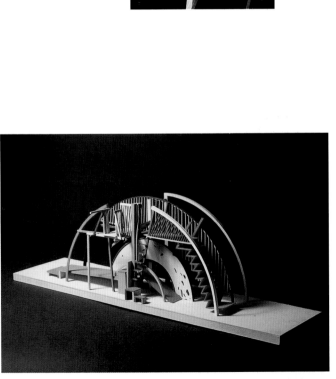

Above: Vlad Kirpichev, *Veranda for a summer house*, 1990, project (in collaboration with Liudmila Kirpicheva and Max Baryshnikov).

Above left: Vlad Kirpichev,. *Manifesto*, collage for Mondo Materialis exhibition, New York, 1989 (in collaboration with Liudmila Kirpicheva and Max Baryshnikov).

Left: Vlad Kirpichev, *Multifunctional children's playground*, 1989, project (in collaboration with Liudmila Kirpicheva and Max Baryshnikov).

SELECTED BIBLIOGRAPHY

Akchurin, Marat, ed. *A Double Rainbow.* Moscow: Molodaya Gvardiya, 1988.

Architecture de Papier d'URSS, exh. cat. Paris: Editions de Regard, 1988.

Art Into Life: Russian Constructivism 1914–1932, exh. cat. New York: Rizzoli, 1990.

Barron, Stephanie and Maurice Tuchman, eds. *The Avant-garde in Russia, 1910–1930: New Perspectives.* Cambridge: The MIT Press, 1980.

Berger, John. *Art and Revolution.* New York: Pantheon, 1969.

Chernevich, Elena. *Soviet Commercial Design of the Twenties.* New York: Abbeville, 1987.

Dabrowski, Magdalena. *Liubov Popova.* New York: The Museum of the Modern Art, 1991.

Ginzburg, Moisei. *Style and Epoch.* Cambridge: The MIT Press, 1982.

Golomstock, Igor. *Totalitarian Art.* New York: Harper Collins, 1990.

Gozak, Andrei and Andrei Leonidov. *Ivan Leonidov.* London: Academy Editions, 1987.

Gray, Camilla. *The Great Experiment: Russian Art 1863–1922.* London, 1962.

Harvard University Art Museums and Busch-Resinger Museum. *El Lissitzky 1890–1941.* Cambridge: Harvard University, 1987.

Ikonnikov, Andrey. *Soviet Architecture Today: 1960s to the E arly 1970s.* Leningrad: Aurora Art Publishers, 1975.

Kantor, Karl. *Krasota i Polza.* Moscow: Iskusstvo, 1967.

Kazimir Malevich: 1878–1935, exh. cat. Los Angeles: The Armand Hammer Museum of Art and Cultural Center, 1990.

Khan-Magomedov, Selim O. *Pioneers of Soviet Architecture.* New York: Rizzoli, 1987.

Khan-Magomedov, Selim O. *Alexander Vesnin and Russian Constructivism.* New York: Rizzoli, 1986.

Khan-Magomedov, Selim O. *Rodchenko: The Complete Work.* Edited by Vieri Quilici. Cambridge: The MIT Press, 1987.

Klotz, Heinrich and Alexander Rappaport. *Paper Architecture: New Projects from the Soviet Union.* New York: Rizzoli, 1990.

Kopp, Anatole. *Town and Revolution.* New York: George Brazilier, 1970.

Lavrentiev, Alexandr. *Varvara Stepanova: The Complete Work.* Edited by John E. Bowlt. Cambridge: The MIT Press, 1988.

Lobanov-Rostovsky, Nina. *Revolutionary Ceramics: Soviet Porcelain 1917–1927.* New York: Rizzoli, 1990.

Lodder, Christina. *Russian Constructivism.* New Haven: Yale University Press, 1983.

Milner, John. *Vladimir Tatlin and the Russian Avant-garde.* New Haven: Yale University Press, 1983.

Models of "Agitarch," exh. cat. Cologne: Linssen Gallery, 1990.

Nesbitt, Lois E. *Brodsky & Utkin.* New York: Princeton Architectural Press and Ronald Feldman Fine Arts, 1991.

Nostalgia of Culture: Contemporary Soviet Visionary Architecture. London: The Architectural Association, 1988.

Paperny, Vladimir. *Kultura Dva.* Ann Arbor: Ardis, 1985.

Sanderson, Warren, ed. *International Handbook of Contemporary Developments in Architecture.* Westport and London: Greenwood Press, 1981.

Shvidkovsky, O.A., ed. *Building in the USSR 1917–1932.* New York: Praeger Publishers, 1971.

Starr, Frederic. *Melnikov, Solo Architect in a Mass Society.* Princeton: Princeton University Press, 1978.

Tupitsyn, Margarita. *Margins of Soviet Art.* Milan: Giancarlo Politi Editore, 1989.

INDEX

DATE